Involving Senior Citizens in Group Music Therapy

of related interest

Group and Individual Work with Older People
A practical guide to running successful activity-based programmes
Swee Hong Chia, Julie Heathcote and Jane Marie Hibberd
Illustrated by Andy Hibberd
ISBN 978 1 84905 128 6
eISBN 978 0 85700 317 1

Connecting through Music with People with Dementia
A guide for caregivers
Robin Rio
ISBN 978 1 84310 905 1
eISBN 978 1 84642 725 1

Group Music Activities for Adults with Intellectual and Developmental Disabilities
Maria Ramey
ISBN 978 1 84905 857 5
eISBN 978 0 85700 434 5

The Creative Arts in Dementia Care
Practical person-centred approaches and ideas
Jill Hayes with Sarah Povey
Foreword by Shaun McNiff
ISBN 978 1 84905 056 2
eISBN 978 0 85700 251 8

Songwriting
Methods, techniques and clinical applications for music therapy clinicians, educators and students
Edited by Felicity Baker and Tony Wigram
Foreword by Even Ruud
ISBN 978 1 84310 356 1
eISBN 978 1 84642 144 0

INVOLVING SENIOR CITIZENS IN GROUP MUSIC THERAPY

JOSEPH PINSON

Jessica Kingsley *Publishers*
London and Philadelphia

First published in 2013
by Jessica Kingsley Publishers
116 Pentonville Road
London N1 9JB, UK
and
400 Market Street, Suite 400
Philadelphia, PA 19106, USA

www.jkp.com

Library of Congress Cataloging in Publication Data
Pinson, Joe.
Involving senior citizens in group music therapy / Joseph Pinson.
p. cm.
Includes bibliographical references and index.
ISBN 978-1-84905-896-4 (alk. paper)
1. Music therapy for older people. I. Title.
ML3920.P565 2013
615.8'51540846--dc23
2012030241

British Library Cataloguing in Publication Data
A CIP catalogue record for this book is available from the British Library

ISBN 978 1 84905 896 4
eISBN 978 0 85700 633 2

Printed and bound in Great Britain

*To my wife, Sara, who provided continuing encouragement,
helpful suggestions and considerable editorial assistance
and
To Betty, whose keen sense of humor, youthful exuberance
and positive attitude regarding the process of aging kept me
coming back for more.*

Contents

List of Songs

Preface

This book is written for professional music therapists, volunteer musicians, caregivers, and family members who serve in behalf of senior citizens in residential facilities. Music therapists provide training for others who may be interested in using music in a beneficial way.

The title for this book was chosen because I am convinced that in some instances music therapists do not "involve" participants fully in the music making process. The adjective "group" is included, because that is the way most services are delivered to seniors, and because most of the methods that I describe would probably not be suitable for hospice care.

Because of the limitations that are part of the aging process, music therapists must:

1. choose or create music that is accessible to most persons

2. design strategies that utilize music skills, cognitive skills, motor skills and social-emotional skills to the fullest

3. present strategies in ways that emphasize having a good time in the moment with results that last

4. develop a good understanding of the challenges that face seniors once they are part of an institutional setting (assisted living and nursing care).

With regard to the first premise, simplicity is critical. Most of the songs that seniors may remember are not that easy to sing. Singing with word sheets in a large font is an option, but what we really need are songs that can be sung without significant prompts after hearing them one or two times. These are similar to the songs that we teach young children, but the content must be something that speaks to the adult experiences of the participants, and more specifically to the experience of seniors in residential facilities. Many music therapists are intimidated by the idea of writing their own songs, but this skill is greatly needed because of the limited number of "standard" songs that meet the guidelines of simplicity and accessibility.

With regard to the second premise, it is not enough just to get seniors to sing. They should be engaged (making music) with song forms that are accessible, with words that have real meaning for them in the present moment (cognitive skills), with songs that incorporate movement and/or the use of hand-held instruments (motor skills) and with songs that emphasize the shared common interests of the group (social skills).

The third premise has to do with the therapist getting beyond just going through the routine of delivering services. It means forming friendships between the provider and those served. Oh—someone will say, we can't be "friends" with our clientele. That would be a conflict of interest. Nonsense! What do they expect us to do—to try to engage members of the group in genuine music making without ever smiling, without ever telling them about our day, without ever making fun of ourselves, or without ever developing a real interest in the lives that they are living at the moment? I tell my students that if you can't have fun providing music therapy services, find another profession. Certainly I am not suggesting that we become like an advocate or family member who works behind the scenes to ensure welfare of an individual—but to form a therapeutic friendship is vital to our success. I also realize that in certain types of clinical relationships the idea of being "friendly" will not work, but the relationship between the music therapist and seniors in residential care is unique and demands a different approach.

The fourth premise really developed from a recent personal situation—being on medical leave in a long-term care hospital. I have been in and around hospitals and residential facilities for all of my career, but only in this experience did I begin to realize the challenges that face those who are confined for any length of time.

When I was a young man, we didn't have "seniors"—or, to put it another way, we didn't call them "seniors." They were "elders" or "old people" or "grandma and grandpa." I don't consider the word itself as applied to this generation to be a real problem, but I do remember a few years ago when a local church promoted their "Senior Sunday" and I thought it was a celebration for guys like me—NO—it was instead a recognition of the "seniors" graduating from local high schools and universities.

Other things have changed. Care of the elderly was at one time the responsibility of the family. In the days when many women did not work outside the home they assumed the role of mother of children and caregiver for older relatives. This was done in the home environment. Persons receiving care were in daily contact with family members.

In the 1940s and 1950s there were no commercial nursing homes. In some cities individuals had turned their larger homes into places that offered care for older citizens. Most of these were substandard and poorly regulated.

The rise of the commercial nursing home industry brought better facilities and increased monitoring by governmental agencies, but they also created places where seniors are usually isolated from family contact except for the times when relatives choose to visit. What was once just a matter of dealing with the problems of aging is now amplified by the loneliness and depression associated with separation from friends and family.

Music therapists who are properly trained can provide interventions that can create a sense of family among the residents of a nursing home, engage persons in a meaningful exchange of ideas that strengthen the concept of community, and help seniors deal with the daily routine of the institutional environment.

In recent months a social worker discovered that equipping an Alzheimer's patient with an iPod usually promoted better attention, better affect, better speech skills, and even improved social skills. This is good news for those who produce and sell these devices, but it is also good news for the seniors who have benefited from this regimen. Should it have been a music therapist who discovered this? Not necessarily—since listening to an iPod is not music therapy—it is therapeutic music. Do music therapists ever prescribe music for listening? Yes—we have been doing it for years. Is it our primary mode of treatment? No.

Just as seniors "feel better" when they listen to recordings of tunes that are meaningful, there is a segment of our society that "feels good" when they make a public statement with their recorded music. When you see a car going down the street with music blaring, the driver is making a statement that says "This is who I am." If you are offended, just be grateful that this person is making a statement with music instead of some more violent or disruptive behavior.

With regard to the isolation and loneliness mentioned previously, I can guarantee that listening to an iPod doesn't make anyone feel less isolated or less lonely. The properly trained music professional can create a music-centered environment where the participants begin to feel part of the community in which they currently reside. They make music together, they share ideas about past and present, and they begin to sense the joy that can be theirs, regardless of the circumstances.

One | *Overview of the Senior Population*

INFORMATION FROM THE CENSUS

According to the United States Census (2010), the population 65 years and over increased at a faster rate (15.1%) than the total United States population (9.7%) during the preceding decade. In addition to growth in the older population, pronounced growth in the male population 65 years and over occurred during the decade.

In spite of the growth of the senior population, there is a smaller percentage of older persons living in nursing homes today than there was in 1965. According to the National Nursing Home Survey (2004) persons 85 and older accounted for less than 16 percent of this segment of the population compared to more than 21 percent in 1985. There seems to be a trend toward the upper-income population moving to assisted living or having their affluent children take care of them. The 2010 census data do not include information about persons in assisted-living facilities.

In our community we have several new facilities for seniors, and in most instances they offer the option of assisted living. In my own practice all of these except two have an assisted living component. In spite of these statistics the number of music therapists working with seniors has increased steadily—in tandem with the rapid increase of that population. Some provide music therapy services exclusively, and others have combined their music therapy skills with the role of activity director. To be able to handle the job of activity director is certainly a plus. The reality is that this responsibility, if done properly, requires a lot of hours—leaving little time to use one's ability as a music therapist.

LIFE EXPECTANCY AND DISABILITY

In the last decade life expectancy in the United States has risen by almost ten years (from 70 to 80). This is a mixed blessing in one sense, since the average person now has more years to possibly face the challenges of dealing with disabling conditions. The World Health Organization (2011) has estimated that 10 percent of the world's population has some form of a disability. As age increases, the percentages go higher (20% of persons whose age is 70+ and 50% of persons whose age is 85+).

Some of the most common causes of disability among seniors include heart disease, stroke, hypertension, cancer, diabetes, pulmonary disease, arthritis, osteoporosis, dementia, depression, visual impairment, and hearing impairment. Any of these conditions may become more critical and debilitating if they result in loss of independence; and this loss is probably one of the major causes of depression among older adults. For one who has led an active life, the idea of dealing with a life of inactivity presents major challenges.

The inactivity itself usually leads to problems with all bodily functions. The phrase "use it or lose it" becomes very real at this stage of life. For some people the idea of retirement means to stop working and take it easy. It may sound like a good plan, but the reality is that your mind and body need to be active to stay healthy. A fall or an illness that leads to several weeks of inactivity is the end of the road for some seniors. It would happen less often if these individuals had something to motivate them to get going again. Persons who were involved in some sort of musical activity as young people should seek out the many opportunities for retirees to participate in bands and choirs designed specifically for those who wish to regain these skills in a meaningful manner. Most of these ensembles are also open to persons who have never played an instrument before. There are exercise groups specifically for seniors, where they not only keep the body working but also meet new friends who motivate them to keep active. There are garden clubs, book clubs and organizations that promote almost any hobby that a senior could have.

Persons who have lived their entire lives with physical limitations caused by crippling disease or accidental injury have in most cases learned to adapt and embrace these conditions. To encounter this kind of loss as a senior, when many other problems are surfacing at the same time, is very difficult if not impossible in some instances. Giving up the automobile, as painful as that may be, is usually something that seniors can learn to accept, but when the lifelong functions of walking, standing, bathing and toileting become too difficult to manage without assistance, there is in many instances a very real tendency to give up on life. When this occurs, depression is usually the outcome.

DEPRESSION AND SENIOR CITIZENS

Doctors are reluctant to diagnose depression because the very mention of the word is itself depressing. Even when diagnosed, some elderly patients may deny the presence of this condition because of the perceived stigma that is attached. Common indicators such as low appetite or difficulty sleeping may be more acceptable as reasons to prescribe possible remedies. Other indicators of depression may be increased anxiety and/or irritability, loss of energy, loss of interest in daily activities, social isolation, and neglect of personal care.

There are several tests that may be administered when caregivers suspect depression in a patient. These include:

1. The Brief Assessment Schedule (BASDEC) has a set of 19 cards with statements from the Schedule. These are presented to the individual with the request to answer "true," "false" or "don't know." Cards are available in various languages, and this method has obvious advantages for persons with hearing impairment. This assessment may be conducted by most staff persons.

2. The Geriatric Depression Scale (GDS) is a self-rating scale that can also be given by interview. There is a 15-item scale and a 30-item scale. The scale is not recommended for persons with cognitive impairment.

3. The Evans Liverpool Depression Rating Scale (ELDRS) is a set of questions referring to the previous four weeks that should rule out depression encountered after admission. It is designed for persons with physical disabilities and may be administered by non-psychiatrically trained staff.

Whether depression is formally diagnosed or not, its symptoms can usually be recognized by most music therapists. During their interaction with a group they will see persons with flat affect, persons who are reluctant to participate, persons who do not make eye contact, persons who do not interact with other group members, and persons whose thoughts seem to be elsewhere.

DEALING WITH A NEW ENVIRONMENT

A great challenge that faces seniors who find themselves in a nursing home environment is adapting to a situation where space is very limited, where strangers abound, and where privacy is minimal. For men or women who have been in the military, or who have survived several years in college dorms, the transition is not so great; but for those who went directly from their first home with mom and dad to a second home of many years with a life mate, the experience can be overwhelming. I have seen persons enter assisted living with all self-help skills intact—only to lose most of those during the first month, causing them to become candidates for transfer to a nursing home. While all of this is happening, age-related lessening of cognitive ability makes it difficult to sort out these changes and cope with them in an appropriate manner. Increased depression may also contribute to less cognitive ability. Some seniors in nursing homes sense that doctors, caregivers, or even close relatives are conspiring to keep them in this new place, and they long for the home environments that are no longer available.

The nursing home brings the challenging of adjusting to a new peer group— something that many persons, old and young, find very difficult. If you have lived your life in an environment of doctors, lawyers, or college professors, it may be a real challenge to accept farmers, truck drivers, and salesmen as your new friends. Upscale nursing homes tend to group higher income folks, but this is not always the case. In some instances persons who lived most of their lives in luxury with high-flying friends find that their retirement plans do not allow this kind of grouping.

Being admitted to a nursing home may be very difficult if there is an unfinished period of grief following the death of a spouse. For those who had a long-term relationship this kind of loss can be very traumatic. The surviving member of this partnership is now faced with making decisions, following daily routines, maintaining family relationships, dealing with financial matters, and numerous situations that were previously approached with two minds instead of one.

The group music therapy experience has been shown to be very valuable in addressing some of the aforementioned problems. It is important for each person living in this new situation to get to know the others who are part of his/her new "family" and to accept them as brothers and sisters. The skilled music therapist can help to create an environment where this kind of bonding is possible. The shared musical experience is the catalyst. Cohen, Bailey, and Nilsson (2002) found that music is very important to seniors, and they studied the optimum level of access to music services. They proposed that increasing access to relevant music experiences through singing, playing instruments, musical training, and the work of music therapists may help maintain and augment quality of life in later years.

Some facilities have locked security doors to prevent persons in more advanced stages of dementia from wandering. Even if the doors are not locked, there is still a sense of confinement. Lack of mobility and/or a sense of the unpredictable nature of what lies outside the door will keep most residents whose cognitive abilities are intact from leaving. I am always intrigued by stories from prisoner-of-war camps and prisons that tell about how individuals invented their own world of activity amidst extreme conditions. Seniors in nursing homes face no such conditions, and the ability of each person to find ways to keep the mind and body occupied are critical to longevity and quality of life.

SUMMARY OF CHAPTER 1

The latest census shows that the number of persons 65 years and older increased at a faster rate (15.1%) than the total United States population during the preceding decade. In spite of the growth of the senior population, there is a smaller percentage of older persons living in nursing homes today than in 1965. The number of music therapists working with seniors has increased steadily. Some provide music therapy services exclusively, and others have combined their music therapy skills with the role of activity director.

In the last decade, life expectancy in the United States has risen by almost ten years (from 70 to 80). This is a mixed blessing in one sense, since the average person now has more years to possibly face the challenges of dealing with disabling conditions. Some of the most common causes of disability among seniors include heart disease, stroke, hypertension, cancer, diabetes, pulmonary disease, arthritis, osteoporosis, dementia, depression, visual impairment, and hearing impairment. For some the idea of retirement means to stop working and take it easy. It may sound like a good plan, but the reality is that your mind and body need to be active to stay healthy. Persons who were involved in some sort of musical activity as young people should seek out the many opportunities for retirees to participate in bands and choirs designed specifically for those who wish to regain these skills in a meaningful manner. Many of these ensembles also accept persons who have never played an instrument before. As painful as that may be, giving up the automobile is usually something that seniors can learn to accept, but when the lifelong functions of walking, standing, bathing, and toileting become too difficult to manage without assistance, there is in many instances a very real tendency to give up on life. When this occurs, depression is usually the outcome.

Common indicators of depression are low appetite, difficulty sleeping, increased anxiety and/or irritability, loss of energy, loss of interest in daily activities, social isolation, and neglect of personal care. Music therapists will see persons with flat affect, persons who are reluctant to participate, persons who do not make eye contact, persons who do not interact with other group members, and persons whose thoughts seem to be elsewhere.

A great challenge that faces seniors who find themselves in a nursing home environment is adapting to a situation where space is very limited, where strangers abound, and where privacy is minimal. While all of this is happening, age-related lessening of cognitive ability makes it difficult to sort out these changes and cope with them in an appropriate manner. Some seniors in nursing homes sense that doctors, caregivers or even close relatives are conspiring to keep them in this new place, and they long for the home environments that are no longer available. The group music therapy experience has been shown to be very valuable in addressing some of the problems related to the residential environment. It is important for each person living in this new situation to get to know the others who are part of his/her new "family" and to accept them as brothers and sisters. The skilled music therapist can help to create an environment where this kind of bonding is possible.

Two | Assessment, Goals, and Objectives

MUSIC THERAPY ASSESSMENT DEFINED

Wigram and Gold (2006) have stated that music therapy assessment evaluates more than just social engagement. The therapist should analyze musical events and musical behaviors that occur during the course of treatment. Assessment is a continuing process that allows the music therapist to continually refine his/her technique to better meet the needs of clientele.

Without proper assessment we cannot address the needs of each individual. It is the first and one of the most important steps in effective music therapy intervention.

Certainly the skills of listening and observation are key to assessing the needs of persons to whom we provide services. I have been a keen observer since I was a young man. I can remember watching every move made by the "special people" in our small city in east Texas. I was fascinated by everything they said and did. It was not morbid curiosity—just fascination. At the time I did not know that there were any career paths associated with this sort of fascination. When I arrived at the point in my life when I began offering music therapy services to persons with special needs, it was a great homecoming for me.

Assessment is usually done on an individual basis, even though services will probably be provided in a group setting. It may not be possible to address the specific needs of each person, so the music therapist may need to prioritize individual objectives for those who appear to have the most difficulty in the group.

Effective assessment is the first step in protocol planning (Michel and Pinson 2005, 2012) that is a regimen for prioritizing needs in an orderly manner. The assessment includes all information that is available to the therapist, planning for intervention, establishing goals and objectives, and measuring progress when intervention begins. Assessment continues throughout the time that services are delivered. It also includes information from other related therapies (speech therapy, occupational therapy, physical therapy, etc.). When we are aware of the interventions of others we can create an atmosphere of cooperation to achieve the best results.

All phases of assessment and treatment should be guided by the Iso-Principle that allows the therapist to be more aware of the present capabilities of each individual and to better plan for services that will facilitate progress in areas of need. Assessment is also a form of accountability that is part of the therapist's need to be ethically responsible to the individual in treatment.

THE INGREDIENTS OF ASSESSMENT

Initial assessment begins during the very first meeting. A more formal evaluation may follow, but these are the things that the therapist should look for from the beginning. Here are some possible *qualitative* observations:

1. *Motor skills*: Was the individual able to participate in simple activities such as clapping hands and making basic movements when requested? Was the individual able to play hand-held rhythm instruments and to pass same to a neighbor in the group?

2. *Communication skills*: Was the individual able to repeat and sing words to simple songs? Was the individual able to answer basic questions about life experience?

3. *Cognitive skills*: Was the individual able to understand directions from the therapist? Was the individual able to give basic information such as name and place of birth?

4. *Social/emotional skills*: Was the individual attentive to others in the group? Was the individual supportive of the needs of others in the group?

These are all objective observations based upon what has transpired during the very first session. It is also important for the music therapist to make personal note of his/her subjective impressions. The intuitive feelings of a trained therapist would not become part of a written assessment but may provide a perspective that is important to the treatment process.

As these subjective impressions are formed, it is important for the music therapist to avoid the idea of comparing this information to that gained in similar encounters with other clientele. One might be thinking, "I have seen this before and know where this is going." True—you may have seen similar behaviors, but it is important to remember that every individual we serve is uniquely different; therefore to make assumptions about the outcome of therapy would be setting up a situation in which you would be less dedicated to proper treatment. Such an attitude might also set the stage for a self-fulfilling prophecy to take control.

As the music therapist gets to know the individuals in the group, there are also some questions that lend themselves to numerical measures. Here are some possible *quantitative* observations:

1. *Motor skills*: How many times did an individual imitate the rhythmic cues of the therapist correctly? How many seconds did the individual play the claves in sync with the beat without interruption?

2. *Communication skills*: How many times did an individual begin singing at the proper moment when directed by the therapist? How many times was the individual able to repeat phrases of a song correctly when requested by the therapist?

3. *Cognitive skills*: How many times did an individual play his/her instrument out of turn? How many times did an individual improvise original rhythms while the group was playing?

4. *Social/emotional skills*: How many times did an individual refuse to join the group in a music activity? How many times did an individual make negative comments during the group session?

Such precise measurements may not be possible if the music therapist is working alone, and this is often why group objectives are used instead of individual objectives.

In the nursing home setting the music therapist may encounter persons who are victims of stroke that renders them unable to use one side of the body. The ability to ambulate may be assessed, but it is not usually something that affects the delivery of music therapy services.

In the area of communication skills we may encounter persons who can no longer speak as a result of some medical situation. In our present society it is not unusual to have persons in the group for whom English is a second language. In this instance the therapist should make every effort to learn key words in the native language to allow these persons to participate.

Cognitive skills may in some instances be greatly impaired. Even when a person does not understand all directions and is unable to respond to questions during the session, he/she may still benefit from the social-emotional connections that are part of the music therapy experience.

Aside from these more obvious and more measurable skill areas the music therapist should be aware of other indicators such as affect, eye contact, making conversation before and after sessions, willingness to help others and anything that might indicate a person's level of comfort in his/her present environment. Those who have a flat affect, who have difficulty making eye contact, and who show other indications of feeling like an outsider are probably the ones who need the most help. Changes in these behaviors do not usually occur quickly, but if the more isolated persons continue to attend, you will probably see gradual improvement.

Michel and Pinson (2005, 2012) spoke to the idea that stress plays an important part in the onset of disease, disorder, and disability. Certainly, seniors in nursing homes are experiencing a lot of stress related to their new location, their loss of independence and, in some cases, grieving over the loss of a spouse. Another contributor to stress is the decrease in hormones that affects all of us as we grow older. Stress is difficult to diagnose and probably even more difficult to manage, but involvement in music has been shown to reduce the level of stress that an individual may experience (Watkins 1997). When seniors are actively engaged in making music together there is distraction and joy in the moment that usually allows them to at least temporarily lay aside some of the workings of the mind that cause stress.

A facility may require an individual assessment for every person in the group. If not, the music therapist should assess those persons who seem to need the most help. There are some formal assessment tools that are available. Coffman (2002) mentions the *Profile of Mood States* (1971), the *Positive and Negative Affect Schedule* PANAS (1988), the *Differential Emotions Scale* (1982), the *Positive States of Mind Scale* PSOM (1988), and the *Philadelphia Geriatric Center Positive and Negative Affect Scales* (1992). These scales have been most used by persons doing research, where the measurement between pre-test and post-test must be accurate to give the data more reliability.

The individual music therapist in most instances will use a much less formal assessment tool that is designed to provide information at the beginning of treatment. This information becomes the basis of goals and objectives that include their own measurement criteria. Here is an assessment tool that has been used with several different populations including seniors. The information contained therein is a composite from several actual case studies:

Sample music therapy assessment

CLIENT	THERAPIST	DATE
J. B.	*J. W. P.*	*XX/XX/2010*

BACKGROUND INFORMATION

J. B. is an 82-year-old female who began living at this nursing facility after the death of her husband. She is a former elementary school teacher who played the piano as a youngster. Before the death of her husband they were both in an assisted living facility. She has no significant health problems but is experiencing some difficulty with ambulation. Some cognitive impairment has been noted.

PROFILE OF CURRENT MUSIC SKILLS IN THE GROUP

1. *Listening: J. B. listens politely to music presented by the therapist, and she does not interrupt, even though some of the music offered does not measure up to her classical tastes.*

2. *Moving: J. B. imitates movements correctly most of the time, but her movements occasionally seem a bit rigid.*

3. *Playing: J. B. plays rhythm instruments when directed. She is always in sync with the beat and improvises new rhythms occasionally.*

4. *Singing: J. B. has a nice voice and sings during most of the songs presented by the therapist.*

PROFILE OF SKILLS OTHER THAN MUSIC

1. *Motor skills: J. B. uses a walker to travel to and from the music group. Her fine motor skills seem to be unimpaired.*

2. *Cognition: J. B. is occasionally confused about day and time, and she usually does not remember what happened during the last meeting of the group.*

3. *Communication skills: J. B. speaks in complete sentences, but she sometimes has difficulty hearing what is said in the group.*

4. *Social/emotional skills: J. B. smiles occasionally, but her affect is flat much of the time. She does not interact very much with others in the music group.*

POSITIVE TRAITS

J. B. has good fine motor skills, good communication skills, and good music skills.

AREAS OF NEED

J. B. has needs in the areas of cognitive skills, and social-emotional skills.

RECOMMENDED INTERVENTION

It is recommended that J. B. participate in the weekly music therapy group, where strategies will address her diminishing cognitive skills and her social-emotional skills.

> *Goal 1: J. B. will make progress or maintain her skill level in the area of cognitive skills.*
>
> *Related objective: When given the opportunity, J. B. will give an informed response during the question/answer song for 15 of 15 sessions by May 1, 20XX.*
>
> *Goal 2: J. B. will make progress or maintain her skill level in the area of social-emotional skills.*
>
> *Related objective: When given the opportunity, J. B. will shake hands with two other persons during the welcome song for 15 of 15 sessions by May 1, 20XX.*

Services should be provided by a board-certified music therapist as a direct agent to J. B. or as a supervising consultant to caregivers. Services will be evaluated continually to insure that the objectives are being met. If progress or maintenance are not achieved, the therapist will adjust the strategies or change the objectives.

(signature)
J. P., MT- BC—January 1, 20XX

It is important to get as much background information as possible. Medical records are not always available, but most participants will answer questions and tell the therapist about themselves. Regarding the case of J. B., I discovered in talking with her that her late husband was a physician in the community. When they married, she retired from teaching to be a full-time homemaker. They had many friends in the medical community and had great times entertaining others in their home. They were both great fans of the symphony and the opera. Before transferring to this facility she and her husband were in an assisted living facility. As previously stated, most seniors are happy to discuss their lives—sometimes offering more detail that one wants. This sort of conversation between therapist and the individual served is not only useful in planning, but it gives the senior an outlet that contributes to the therapeutic process.

The assessment speaks about the "positive traits" and also about the "areas of need." The focus is really on the former, because the abilities that a person displays at time of assessment are very often the key to treating conditions of disability.

Note that in the goals I have used the phrase "will make progress or maintain" certain skills, because the reality of the senior population is that they are in a period of decline—regardless of the medical and therapeutic measures that may be administered. In the absence of real progress, maintaining a skill is a very acceptable outcome. In some instances decline will occur in spite of all that doctors and therapists can do.

It is possible that this assessment may be read by no one but the music therapist; however, the language should be clear, and the objectives should be stated in terms that most everyone can understand. The use of the individual's name throughout the document is intentional to let others know that she has great value in the eyes of the therapist.

As mentioned in the assessment, "services will be evaluated continually"—which means, to the music therapist, that assessment continues, even as the intervention is being activated.

Group objectives are often used in music therapy with seniors. These are formed on the basis of the information received from individual assessments and the observations of the therapist.

GOALS AND OBJECTIVES

A music therapy *goal* is a direction for treatment. It is usually a very general statement that includes:

1. the name of the individual in treatment

2. the phrase "will make progress" or "will maintain skills"

3. an area of treatment (motor skills, communication skills, cognitive skills, and social-emotional skills).

Sometimes agencies set goals with more specific outcomes and specific times of completion, but I prefer the general, open-ended statement that gives us "direction" without locking in to an outcome that is usually nothing more than speculation.

One of J. B.'s goals was to "make progress or maintain her skill level in the area of cognitive skills." Another goal was to "make progress or maintain her skill level in the area of social-emotional skills."

A music therapy *objective* is an immediate focus of treatment. It usually includes a specific measurable outcome, a criterion for attaining the outcome, and a projected time of completion.

With regard to the first goal for J. B., I developed a complementary objective that said she would "give an informed response during the question/answer song for 15 of 15 sessions by May 1, 20XX." I set the criteria at "15 of 15" because I knew that she was capable of this kind of response. At the time I drafted the objective (after the second session) she was scoring "2 of 2," so my objective was really in the direction of her maintaining this skill level.

With regard to J. B.'s second goal, I developed an objective that said she would "shake hands with two other persons during each session." Her level of achievement was only "1 of 2" after the first session, because she was reluctant to participate. The objective asks for "15 of 15," so in this instance I was really looking for improvement in this social skill. Obviously, a good social relationship with other group members is much more than shaking hands, but this is very measurable, and its accomplishment could lead to other positive behaviors in the area of group interaction.

Taking into consideration factors of time and available resources, it is sometimes advantageous to consider a group objective. The objective set for J. B. regarding cognitive skills could be adapted for a group. As a group objective it would probably be stated this way: Members of the music therapy group will give an informed response during the question/answer song for 15 of 15 sessions by May 1, 20XX. Reporting would probably be a percentage of persons responding appropriately at each session.

J. B.'s objective regarding social-emotional skills could also be adapted as a group objective that could be stated in this way: During the welcome song members of the group will shake hands with two other persons per session by May 1, 20XX. This would also be measured as a percentage of those participating.

It is obvious that "answering a question" or "shaking hands" is only a very small part of what goes on at each session, and neither of these really measures cognitive skills or social emotional skills to the fullest extent. These objectives only represent a sample of progress or maintenance of the goal areas. At all times the music therapist is looking for all indicators that would translate to quality of life for the individuals involved. Most of the documentation regarding sessions includes a narrative that can point to other things that were noted during each meeting.

Assessment is more fully described as two concentric circles that move together through the treatment cycle. One circle represents responses of the person(s) in therapy, and the other represents the feelings and thoughts of the therapist. Constant assessment, re-assessment and adjustment of both circles during treatment will create a climate in which music therapy can be most effective (Michel and Pinson 2005, 2012).

Once treatment begins, measuring objectives becomes a real challenge for the music therapist, especially if he/she works alone. If an assistant is available, that person may take data on each individual as the session progresses. Therapists who work alone usually employ a "planned activity check" that allows them to take group data at a particular moment or moments during the session.

SUMMARY OF CHAPTER 2

Music therapy assessment evaluates more than just social engagement. The therapist records information about musical events and musical behaviors that may assist him/her in providing treatment. Assessment is a continuing process that allows for continual refinement during the course of treatment. It is usually done on an individual basis, even though services for seniors will probably be provided in a group setting. Effective assessment is the first step in protocol planning (Michel and Pinson 2005, 2012) that is a regimen for prioritizing needs in an orderly manner. It also includes information from other related therapies (speech therapy, occupational therapy, physical therapy, etc.). Assessment is a form of accountability that is part of the therapist's need to be ethically responsible to the individual in treatment.

Initial assessment begins during the very first meeting. A more formal evaluation may follow, but these are the things that the therapist should look for from the beginning:

1. motor skills

2. communication skills

3. cognitive skills

4. social/emotional skills.

These are all objective observations based upon what has transpired during the very first session. It is also important for the music therapist to make personal note of his/her subjective impressions. We look for information that is qualitative (describing the various levels of participation in activities presented during the assessment) and quantitative (observations that include numerical data regarding the responses during assessment). Aside from these more obvious and more measurable skill areas the music therapist should be aware of other indicators such as affect, eye contact, making conversation before and after sessions, willingness to help others, and anything that might indicate a person's level of comfort for his/her present environment. Michel and Pinson (2005, 2012) spoke to the idea that stress plays an important part in the onset of disease, disorder, and disability. Certainly, seniors in nursing homes are experiencing a lot of stress related to their new location, their loss of independence and, in some cases, grieving over the loss of a spouse. There are some formal assessments of stress that are available, but in most cases the individual music therapist will use a much less formal tool that is designed to provide information at the beginning of treatment.

The text provides a sample assessment that includes background information, profile of current music skills in the group, a profile of skills other than music, a list of positive traits, a list of areas of need, recommendations, goals, and related objectives. It is important to get as much background information as possible. Medical records are not always available, but most participants will answer questions and tell the therapist about themselves. The focus is on the positive traits, because the abilities that a person displays at the time of assessment are very often the key to treating conditions of disability. There is intentional use of the individual's name throughout the document to let others know that he/she has great value in the eyes of the therapist.

A music therapy goal is a direction for treatment. It is usually a very general statement that includes:

1. the name of the individual in treatment

2. the phrase "will make progress" or "will maintain skills"

3. an area of treatment (motor skills, communication skills, cognitive skills, and social-emotional skills).

A music therapy objective is an immediate focus of treatment. It usually includes a specific measurable outcome, a criterion for attaining the outcome, and a projected time of completion.

Assessment is more fully described as two concentric circles that move together through the treatment cycle. One circle represents responses of the person(s) in therapy, and the other represents the feelings and thoughts of the therapist (Michel and Pinson 2005, 2012).

Three | Current Music Therapy Interventions

INTERVENTIONS FROM THE LITERATURE

Much has been done to serve the needs of seniors in nursing homes and assisted living facilities. Belgrave *et al.* (2011) have listed 12 interventions, the following is a paraphrase of material from their book:

1. Gait training and music has been especially effective with persons recovering from a stroke. Michael Thaut and associates at Colorado State University have developed a regimen known as Rhythmic Auditory Stimulation in which the rhythm and tempo of music composed specifically for this purpose is used as an auditory cue for progressive rehabilitation. This technique is best suited to use with individuals and is aimed at improving motor skills for seniors.

2. Imagery with music, also known as Guided Imagery and Music, developed by Helen Bonny (1921-2010), is a technique that uses recorded music chosen for its ability to elicit relaxation and imagery. It can allow participants to explore memories with the guidance of a counselor that may be important to quality of life and healing.

3. Instrument play can provide a successful musical experience for seniors. Hand-held instruments (claves, maracas, tubular shakers, hand drums, wood blocks, tambourines, etc.) work well with this population. It has been noted that a hand drum placed in the lap of an individual in treatment will create additional vibrations that may lead to a higher rate of participation. When an individual has use of only one hand, a single maraca may be used, or a clave struck against a wheel chair may provide a means of rhythmic expression. Electronic devices are available that will ring a bell, strike a drum, or shake a tambourine.

4. Iso-Principle, developed by Ira Altschuler (1948), uses music to match the present state of an individual, followed by changes in the music aimed at improving mood and behavior. Nearly everything we do in music therapy involves the use of Iso-Principle. To determine and match the mood, the intelligence, the attitude, the physical capacity, and all facets of an individual are a first step toward treatment. We cannot take a person to a new place until we first determine "where he/she is at" in the present moment. For seniors who are agitated this principle may be used to bring them to a more relaxed state. The opposite might be true for those who are sedentary and lacking normal affect. Iso-Principle is also used in gait training and instrument play following the determination of a baseline for treatment.

5. Life review with music, or music cued reminiscence, is used to increase recall in seniors. Music may provide the structure that will allow a person in some stage of dementia to recall certain events from earlier life. If the person has some musical training or a strong affinity for music, the music may help bring back many memories, but even for the average non-musical individual, music has probably had a strong influence on his/her life. Music cued reminiscence may be used in the context of a group, and each person will probably have different recollections. Because of varying ages in music therapy groups, the therapist will try to choose something that bridges the life spans of the persons involved. Life review with music is usually employed in an individual session. In this setting the music is chosen according to requests of the individual or information from family members.

6. Living legacy project may take on different forms. It could be a CD or DVD of the patient and therapist singing familiar songs. It could be a scrapbook (electronic or hard copy) that includes photos, articles, or stories important to the individual and family. This type of intervention is only possible in individual sessions. Advances in electronic recording and editing have made this strategy more accessible.

7. Movement to music has been found to be more effective than exercise regimens without the musical component. Recorded music may be used for this type of intervention, but Cevasco and Grant (2003) found that the highest levels of participation occurred during unaccompanied singing or sounds of the djembe. The conclusion was that additional accompaniment provides too much auditory stimulation. Holmes *et al.* (2006) found that 69 percent of the persons involved in their study showed a significant increase in levels of participation when the stimulus was live music, compared to only 25 percent with recorded music and 12.5 percent with silence.

8. Music listening can be very beneficial to seniors at all stages of decline, especially if the preferences of persons in treatment are taken into consideration. New technology has made this type of intervention much easier to implement—even on an individual basis with the use of headphones. Studies have shown that listening to recorded music decreased disruptive behaviors in persons who have Alzheimer's disease.

9. Progressive muscle relaxation with music has been used to decrease pain perception, agitation and anxiety—resulting in increased relaxation. Pairing these techniques with music provides additional benefits because of the heightened level of attention and participation. The benefits of relaxation include decreased blood pressure, decreased heart and respiratory rate, relief from anxiety, and depression agitation. General stress reduction improves coping skills and promotes better adjustment to social situations.

10. Sensory stimulation and music occurs in most music therapy interventions that involve singing and playing instruments. Even a person who has impaired vision and hearing may benefit from the tactile stimulation that is part of playing an instrument. Music can increase vocalization, because the rhythm in speech is closely akin to that in music. Maximum stimulation is achieved by using a wide variety of pitched instruments. Drums provide a tactile experience as well as the benefits of the sound vibrations. Singing and free vocalization can increase voice production that in most cases encourage socialization.

11. Songwriting can be an effective means of engaging an individual or a group in composing lyrics to fit a familiar tune or one provided by a music therapist. A story offered by a participant might also be converted to a song. The therapist needs to be well acquainted with song forms, and the lyrics that are developed should be simple and accessible. Songs may be developed that allow the clientele to fill in the blanks to express ideas. Some seniors may be able to accompany themselves in a rendition of a song that has been created. In most instances the music therapist will provide the accompaniment.

12. Therapeutic singing uses songs preferred by seniors. The therapist presents these and encourages participants to sing along. Even if a person is unable to sing, he/she may benefit from this review of music that is probably still in the memory bank. Seniors with diminishing cognitive abilities may not be able to remember the names of songs, but if the therapist searches for tunes that were popular during the senior's younger years, they will probably be able to sing along on many of them.

INTERVENTIONS FROM MY EXPERIENCE

During my several years of working with seniors I have observed and sometimes used some of the following:

1. The welcome song has been a part of group music therapy sessions for as long as I can remember, but the emphasis has usually been on the idea of the therapist offering a musical welcome to participants. It can and should be extended to become an activity in which all participants welcome one another in a real group experience. It should also be a time of learning names (for the therapist and the clientele) and reinforcing that learning with music. There will be more about this in Chapter 5.

2. Playing hand-held chimes can be very effective if the cognitive and physical ability of group members allows them to play a chime when cued by the therapist. The therapist can use an electronic keyboard to create an interesting accompaniment to familiar tunes, allowing him/her to be able to cue the entrance of chimes. This type of activity may even become a vehicle for performance for other residents, or a combined performance with a visiting bell or chime choir.

3. The parachute activity that borders on recreation therapy has been used effectively in groups of seniors. A regular parachute or therapeutic parachute with special handles may be used by seniors in a circle. Use of this type of intervention is dependent upon the physical capabilities of group members. A musical accompaniment may enhance this experience.

4. The old fishing pole allows each member of the group to use a pole with attached line to go fishing in a box that contains cardboard fish with names of songs. Once the catch has been made, the group sings the song designated by the fish.

5. The modified bull horn (with crazy, distorted sounds) may allow each member of the group to express frustrations in a way that no one is offended. This might be done in the context of a song that says:

Now Hear This!

> *Now hear this! (clap-clap-clap) Now hear this! (clap-clap-clap)*
> *I'm gonna tell it (clap-clap-clap)—like it is! (clap-clap-clap)*
> *What I say (clap-clap-clap)—on this day (clap-clap-clap)*
> *is none (clap-clap-clap)—none of your biz! (clap-clap-clap)*

> *[Joseph Pinson © 2012]*

In this version I would have the group sing through the song and follow with an instrumental interlude during which each person took a turn at the bull horn. I haven't used this for a while, but it was always a lot of fun.

6. The art gallery is an activity in which the therapist presents each person with a small stack of US letter-size representations of various paintings. After the choice is made, the therapist asks each person to describe the painting and tell what it means to him/her. A song between selections might say something like what follows.

Everyone is Different

Everyone is diff'rent. That is plain to see.
Everyone is diff'rent. That is plain to see.
There's no one else like you. There's no one else like me.
Everyone is diff'rent. That is plain to see.

[Joseph Pinson © 2012]

7. Name that tune allows seniors to name a song presented by the therapist as soon as they recognize it. If this activity is used with a group, the therapist should divide the participants into two teams. It can be a game to see which team does the best. As soon as each song is identified, the therapist should pass out word sheets (large font) in order that the song may be sung by the entire group. Following the singing the therapist may want to ask participants what meaning this song has for each of them. Some therapists have adapted tune recognition into a sort of musical bingo in which participants put a marker on the tune name when it is played or performed by the therapist. This strategy demands that participants be able to read and recognize the information in order to play. In my opinion it would be less effective than the team approach.

8. The closing song is just as the name indicates—a way of wrapping up the session. Many times, when time was running out, I have just passed out word sheets for "Happy Trails" by Dale Evans Rogers (1951). Most seniors remember this tune from radio and television in the late 1940s and early 1950s. In a later chapter you will find suggestions about other songs and strategies for closing.

OUR SERVICES IN COMPARISON

It is useful to look through the preceding list to make comparisons with what seniors are receiving from other therapeutic disciplines and also from activity directors in nursing homes. It is not to say that any duplication of services is a bad thing, but it is important for music therapists to consider strategies that are unique to our discipline, because that increases our job security and also lets the public know that what we offer is above and beyond the things seniors receive on a fairly routine basis.

Gait training is primarily a responsibility of the physical therapist. Some physical therapists use music with their interventions, but none of them use it in the way that Michael Thaut suggests. If the music therapist offers this service, administrators may sense that it is a duplication of what physical therapists provide.

Guided Imagery and Music is certainly the domain of professional music therapists, and more specifically those who are also licensed professional counselors.

Instrument play is often used by activity directors. All that is required is a set of rhythm instruments, a boom-box, and someone who knows how to give start and stop. Since participants know to start when the music starts and stop when the music stops, leadership is probably not a priority. This is not a criticism of the work of activity directors, but as you will see in reading further, trained music therapists or even music volunteers can make this activity much more purposeful and engaging.

The Iso-Principle is certainly a part of every music therapist's training, and rightly so, because it was developed by a man who was himself a music therapist; however, the basic idea of starting a journey from your present location and moving toward a destination falls into the area of common sense. I am thinking that anyone who has contact with seniors in a residential setting has some of this.

Life review with music, or music cued reminiscence, could be done by most anyone who can assemble appropriate recordings and lead a discussion regarding the content. It is not really a counseling technique but a way of helping an older person connect with some things in life that may have been forgotten.

A living legacy project is something that even a family member could undertake, and, probably, a family member would be the most qualified to do this—having much more access to family history, photographs, and other memorabilia that would make this intervention more effective.

Movement to music is often done by activity directors. Most of them understand that the music should be stimulative, and they have probably found that seniors will move to all kinds of music—not just that of their own generation. Some leadership is required to encourage participants to exercise different parts of the body.

Music listening is certainly something that activity directors and family members may implement. For seniors to listen with some interest the selections should probably be their own or those selected by others that represent their generation. It is an activity that the person in treatment may continue in the privacy of his/her room.

Progressive muscle relaxation would seem to be the domain of the physical therapist, but I believe that most of their work is in the area of helping people regain the use of physical capabilities that may have been lost due to illness or injury. The work of trained music therapists can be very helpful in this area.

Sensory stimulation with music is probably most associated with music therapists. Sensory stimulation alone is the domain of occupational therapists, and I know that some of them also use music as part of their interventions. Occupational therapy and music therapy have a long and productive history of working together to achieve desired results.

Songwriting is probably most associated with music therapy, but I can see that a good songwriter without music therapy training could probably have a significant impact on the needs of an individual.

Therapeutic singing is often done by activity directors and volunteer musicians. It would probably be called a "sing-a-long." Even someone with no music training could probably lead one of these activities with the help of CD accompaniment. There is a fairly large collection of these available from Eldersong Publications (www.eldersong.com).

The welcome song is used by a lot of music therapists, but when I have observed its use, the focus is usually on the therapist offering a musical greeting to the participants—not a strategy in which all persons in the group sing a welcome to one another—something that will be discussed in a later chapter.

Playing hand-held chimes can be a useful activity for a music therapist leading a senior group, but because of the physical and cognitive challenges, it is difficult to always involve all persons. There are hand-held chime choirs for seniors in which the participants actually read printed music. For this kind of group the challenge for the music therapist is to find or arrange pieces that are challenging but accessible. In some instances the music is enlarged to accommodate persons with visual impairment.

The parachute activity is probably the domain of recreation therapists, but it can be used in a music therapy group. The random nature of involvement in bouncing a beach ball up and down makes it very difficult to measure responses.

The modified bull horn is one that I have not seen other therapists use, but I will claim no ownership for the idea. It can be a lot of fun when seniors are encouraged to just say anything that comes to mind without fear of censorship.

The art gallery could certainly be used by activity directors or volunteers. The musical element is not necessary for its success as a vehicle for discussion.

Name that tune could be used by activity directors with a set of CDs that represent songs from the senior generation. It could also be used by volunteer musicians who could perform songs that the seniors might recognize. I don't use this any longer, because it does not get everyone involved in the music making.

The closing song is used by a lot of music therapists but could also be used by volunteer musicians. I must relate a funny story from the days when I served persons with developmental disabilities. My music therapy practice was based in the facility chapel, so it was not unusual for us to use religious songs during some of the sessions. Our closing song was called "God Be With You" (Pinson 1980). One of the residents occasionally got bored or "ready to move on" at the mid-point of the session. Knowing the name of the closing song, he would sometimes suggest, "Let's sing 'God Be With You.'"

WHERE DO WE GO FROM HERE?

The remainder of this book will focus on four of the interventions that have been mentioned: The welcome song, instrument play (incorporated with movement to music), therapeutic singing (utilizing a question/answer technique to stimulate recall and communication) and a closing song that allows as much participation as possible. Some strategies are combined to maintain interest. The Iso-Principle is used throughout to assure that what is presented is accessible. Each person should have a successful musical experience. These will be presented in new ways that promote maximum involvement and improve or maintain cognitive skills, motor skills, and social-emotional skills. In general the strategies presented require some music skills, but they are based on logical principles that a person with some basic training should be able to understand and use.

SUMMARY OF CHAPTER 3

This chapter presents several different interventions that are in current use in the field. These include:

1. *Gait training with music*: music composed specifically for this purpose used as an auditory cue for progressive rehabilitation.

2. *Imagery with music*: a technique that uses recorded music chosen for its ability to elicit relaxation and imagery.

3. *Instrument play*: using hand-held instruments (claves, maracas, tubular shakers, hand drums, wood blocks, tambourines, etc.).

4. *Iso-Principle*: using music to match the present state of an individual, followed by changes in the music aimed at improving mood and behavior.

5. *Life review with music or music cued reminiscence*: providing the structure that will allow a person to recall certain events from earlier life.

6. *Living legacy project*: a CD or DVD of the patient and therapist singing familiar songs, or a scrapbook of memorable events.

7. *Movement to music*: may use CDs, but higher levels of involvement occur during unaccompanied singing or with live accompaniment.

8. *Music listening*: found to be beneficial to seniors at all stages of decline, especially if the preferences of seniors are taken into consideration.

9. *Progressive muscle relaxation with music*: used to decrease pain perception, agitation and, anxiety, resulting in increased relaxation.

10. *Sensory stimulation with music*: usually involves singing and playing instruments—can increase vocalization and encourage socialization.

11. *Songwriting*: effective means of engaging an individual or a group in composing lyrics to fit a familiar tune or one provided by a music therapist.

12. *Therapeutic singing*: using songs preferred by seniors to encourage participation, with live or recorded accompaniment.

13. *The welcome song*: therapist sometimes offering a musical greeting to participants—should be a time of participants actively learning names.

14. *Playing hand-held chimes*: effective if the cognitive and physical ability of group members allows them to play when cued by the therapist.

15. *The parachute activity*: borders on recreation therapy but has been used effectively—good motor skills required.

16. *The old fishing pole*: allowing persons in a group to choose songs by pitching a line into a bucket—one of many ideas used to stimulate interest.

17. *The modified bull horn (with crazy, distorted sounds)*: allows members of the group to express frustrations without offending others.

18. *Art gallery*: using representations of various paintings, asking each person to describe the painting and tell what it means to him/her.

19. *Name that tune*: allows seniors to name a song presented by the therapist as soon as they recognize it: may involve some discussion.

20. *The closing song*: a way of wrapping up the session—usually a familiar song such as "Happy Trails" by Dale Evans Rogers (1951).

It is useful to look through the preceding list to make comparisons with what seniors are receiving from other therapeutic disciplines and also from activity directors in nursing homes. It is not to say that any duplication of services is a bad thing, but it is important for music therapists to consider strategies that are unique to our discipline.

1. Gait training is generally a responsibility of physical therapy. With music (Rhythmic Auditory Stimulation) it is provided by a music therapist.

2. Imagery with music is certainly the domain of professional music therapists who are also trained as professional counselors.

3. Activity directors and music therapists provide instrument play. One purpose of this book is to offer more creative ways of using this activity.

4. The Iso-Principle is a part of every music therapist's training; however, the basic idea is used in many therapeutic modalities.

5. Life review with music or music cued reminiscence could be done by most anyone who can assemble recordings and lead a discussion.

6. A living legacy project is something that even a family member could undertake, and that person would be well qualified.

7. Movement to music is often done by activity directors, who can lead group members to exercise different parts of the body.

8. Music listening may be implemented by activity directors and family members. Seniors may continue this in their rooms.

9. Progressive muscle relaxation would seem to be the domain of physical therapy, but most of their work is in the area of helping people regain the use of physical capabilities. The work of trained music therapists can be very helpful in this area.

10. Sensory stimulation with music is probably most associated with music therapists—usually in cooperation with an occupational therapist.

11. Songwriting is probably most associated with music therapy, but a music therapist might be able to train a volunteer to use this strategy.

12. Therapeutic singing, sometimes called a "sing-along" is often done by activity directors and volunteer musicians.

13. The welcome song is used by a lot of music therapists, but the focus is usually on the therapist offering a musical greeting to the participants.

14. Playing hand-held chimes can be a useful activity offered by a music therapist leading a senior group, if the members have good motor skills.

15. The parachute activity is probably the domain of recreation therapists, but it can also be used in a music therapy group.

16. The modified bull horn could be used by most anyone and can be a lot of fun, when seniors can say anything without fear of censorship.

17. The art gallery could certainly be used by activity directors or volunteers. The musical element is not necessary for its success.

18. Name that tune could be used by activity directors with a set of CDs or by volunteer musicians. Music therapists use this occasionally.

19. The closing song is used by a lot of music therapists but could also be used by volunteer musicians.

The remainder of this book will focus on four of the interventions that have been mentioned:

- the welcome song

- instrument play (incorporated with movement to music)

- therapeutic singing (utilizing a question/answer technique to stimulate recall and communication)

- closing song that allows as much participation as possible.

Four | An Improved Plan of Intervention

THE BASIC PRINCIPLES

My plan for music therapy sessions is based upon some principles that have been around for a long time, but in my own practice and the work of others that I have observed, their incorporation has not always been present:

1. *Live music*: presented as unaccompanied singing or singing with various instrumental accompaniments.

   Rationale: Singing with CDs (aka Karaoke) is a great activity, but it never offers the same level of involvement as singing with live accompaniment or even singing without accompaniment. Singing in the shower is a great exercise (and I hope you don't need a CD to encourage you in that direction).

2. *Multi-tasking*: not always easy for seniors but possible if the demands are kept within a reasonable framework.

   Rationale: Knowing that seniors are capable of multi-tasking, it is imperative that we get them involved in the music making as much as possible; therefore, to ask them to sing and play instruments or to sing and do physical movements is the direction that we should go.

3. *Rhythmic and thematic variation*: not in the formal (classical) sense, but in a way that the average person can feel and appreciate.

   Rationale: The minds of everyone in the western world are programmed to relate to musical variations, whether it is a change of tempo, a change of meter, a melody stated with breaks, or a fermata or crescendo. To give participants less is to cheat them of the musical experience that they deserve.

4. *Topics relevant to the present situation*: not "Who is your favorite movie star?" Who cares? The group wants to know who you are, how you feel, and how they can help you feel better.

   Rationale: If we can assist seniors in residential settings to accept the fact that this is their new home, they will find each day more fulfilling, and their quality of life will be greatly improved. We can sing the old songs and play musical games, but these are only diversions. If our music can allow them to learn more about the other residents (their new family), to learn new ways of coping with the environment, and to learn the joy of making music together, we will have made a great contribution to their daily experience.

5. *Having fun together*: If we aren't having fun, why would we want to come to music therapy?

   Rationale: Seniors have reached a stage in life where a lot of the "fun" things are no longer accessible to them. Making music has no age barrier. I have seen centenarians who still play the piano—and play quite well. Most of the persons in our group are not musicians, but they can still participate in making music together, and if the music therapist is properly trained to provide services, they will have a grand time doing it.

THE ELEMENTS

The welcome song will be presented in a way that allows each participant to learn the names of the others in the group through singing and calling names between each statement of the song. I can remember a time in my career, when I was striving to write a new welcome song for each session, because I knew that the participants would enjoy this. WRONG! It is not about me presenting a performance that they will enjoy. My objective should be to present something in which their participation is maximized. They are the performers. I am the therapist, who is trained to provide them with a successful musical experience. A simple welcome song might go something like this.

It's Good to See You

> George—it's good to see you.
> George—it's good to see you.
> We're glad you came to help us sing and play.
> George—it's good to see you.

[Joseph Pinson © 2012]

Or, if the music therapist wants to include some movement and additional rhythm, the song might look like this:

> *George (clap-clap-clap)—it's good to see you. (clap-clap-clap)*
> *George (clap-clap-clap)—it's good to see you. (clap-clap-clap)*
> *We're glad you came to help us sing and play. (clap-clap-clap)*
> *George (clap-clap-clap)—it's good to see you. (clap-clap-clap)*

Most persons in our society have their names sung to them once a year—on their birthdays. It is one thing to hear someone say "Happy birthday." It is quite another to hear it sung with your name included. Music is very powerful, and sometimes even the people in the business (that's us) overlook that fact. In music therapy the participants hear their names sung to them every week, and they hear the names of all other members of the group with a melody attached that helps them remember. Musical jingles were at one time a very big business, because advertisers knew that linking a message with a melody made it more memorable. In more recent times the music has taken a backseat to the elaborate visuals that we see on television, but it is still present in a more supportive way. Recently, while doing my walking, I saw one of the new cars that they are advertising. I found myself humming and hearing the beat of the hip-hop song used as a background for the commercial. Music is *powerful*—don't ever forget it.

Rationale: The participants are now a part of a new community, whether they accept that fact or not. A first step in joining a new community is to learn the names of your neighbors. In the group we will learn more than just names, but the name is the first step. This activity also provides an excellent way for the therapist to learn names and also become part of the community.

Instrument play (that I prefer to call a structured motor strategy) is much more than my playing music while they play instruments. For maximum involvement seniors should be playing instruments *and* singing. For this purpose the song must be familiar and short (usually just a chorus or refrain, as it is sometimes called). Once we have played and sung the song in a basic rendition, we should explore variations that engage the participants while extending the time of the motor activity. This means that the music therapist must do some creative thinking and planning.

You should also have a back-up plan, in case the original doesn't work. Here is an example of one of the variations that might be used. The participants play their instruments where the claps are indicated.

Crawdad Song

> *You get a line, (clap-clap-clap) and I'll get a pole, (clap-clap-clap)*
> *honey. (clap-clap-clap-clap-clap)*
> *You get a line, (clap-clap-clap) and I'll get a pole, (clap-clap-clap)*
> *babe. (clap-clap-clap-clap-clap)*
> *You get a line, (clap-clap-clap) and I'll get a pole, (clap-clap-clap)*
> *and we'll go down (clap-clap-clap) to the crawdad hole, (clap-clap-clap)*
> *honey, (clap-clap-clap-clap-clap) baby (clap-clap-clap-clap-clap)*
> *mine. (clap-clap-clap-clap-clap) Yea! (clap-clap-clap)*

[Traditional]

Rationale: Playing instruments in the same manner all of the time can be *boring*. You can do it in your sleep (and some individuals do just that). When we sing and play we become an integral part of the performance, and, in general, our interest is maintained at a higher level. Does everyone like variation? Do you always prepare a recipe the same way every time? Variation is part of all of the music that we hear (with the possible exception of the hymns in church on Sunday morning); however, I have seen organists who had the ability to improvise and engage the congregation in a brand new worship experience. Our seniors deserve new musical experiences every time we get together.

Therapeutic singing (that I prefer to call the question/answer song) begins with a song that tells about life experience. It may be a brand new tune (very basic) or a familiar song like "This Little Light of Mine." And someone will say, "That's a children's song. We can't use that with seniors." Of course we can, if we change the words to say:

> *This is what I do—when I'm feeling blue.*
> *This is what I do—when I'm feeling blue.*
> *This is what I do—when I'm feeling blue.*
> *It works for me. It just might work for you.*

When a group member tells us that he likes to read during difficult times, we learn more about him (our brother in the community), and we also learn about a technique that we may want to try one day. Seniors are capable of learning new tunes for this strategy, but these must be constructed in a manner that makes them very accessible.

Rationale: When members of the group share ideas about things such as "feeling blue" that affect their daily lives, the sense of community is greatly enhanced. When they share things that tell us who they are, everyone feels more connected.

Sharing these thoughts in a musical context, where their importance is made more meaningful, makes this an experience that helps to create a foundation for healthy social-emotional skills in the present moment.

The closing song is basically just a way of establishing closure. It is a time in the session where no measurement of skills is taking place. On many occasions I have just passed out word sheets and ask those present to sing along. If time permits I add another song that again recognizes the participants. It is a good time to verbally (or musically) thank everyone for coming to the session and wishing them all good things in the week ahead. No singing is encouraged on this one. It is my farewell message to the group. One of these added songs goes like this.

Thank You for Making Good Music

> *Thank you, George—for making good music.*
> *Thank you, Susan—for making good music.*
> *Thank you, Elizabeth—for making good music.*
> *Your being here has really made my day.*

[Joseph Pinson © 2012]

The song continues until all members of the group have been addressed. If you run out of names in the middle, just sing "Thank you—for making good music" for a phrase or two, and then finish with the last phrase. This song provides a good element of closure and recognizes the contribution of each individual.

Rationale: As in all other parts of the session "ritual" (and it is certainly that), it is important to involve all participants as much as possible in the music making. This might mean, as before, adding some variation to the song, or at least singing it a second time in a new key—something that they instinctively appreciate without knowing why.

With these suggested elements in place the properly trained music therapist can deliver services that engage all seniors in the group in singing, playing instruments, multi-tasking (singing and playing instruments) and having a good time doing it.

When seniors can have fun making music together, it is a real first step toward their building community in their new home. In spite of the work of dedicated staff professionals, a nursing home or assisted living facility is a very impersonal place. It is up to the residents to create their own personal affiliation with others who share their space. The music therapist can play a key role in this transition.

SUMMARY OF CHAPTER 4

The plan for improved services is based upon some principles that have been around for a long time, but their incorporation has not always been present. These include:

1. *Live music*: presented as singing without accompaniment or singing with various instrumental accompaniments.

2. *Multi-tasking*: not always easy for seniors but possible if the demands are kept within a reasonable framework.

3. *Rhythmic and thematic variation*: not in the formal (classical) sense, but in a way that the average person can feel and appreciate.

4. *Topics relevant to the present situation* that allow the group to know who you are, how you feel, and how they can help you feel better.

5. *Having fun together*: if we aren't having fun, why would we want to come to music therapy?

A successful session includes the following elements:

1. *The welcome song*: presented in a way that allows each participant to learn the names of the others in the group through singing and calling names between each statement of the song.

2. *Instrument play*: that I call Structured Motor Strategy, in which group members should be playing instruments and singing a song that is familiar and short, followed by variations that extend the time of the motor strategy

3. *Therapeutic singing*: that I call the question/answer song, which deals with life experience, inside the facility and before the persons were admitted, also performed by the group singing and playing instruments.

4. *The closing song*: a way of establishing closure, thanking everyone for attending and participating, and wishing them all good things in the week ahead.

With these suggested elements in place the properly trained music therapist can deliver services that engage all seniors in the group in singing, playing instruments, multi-tasking (singing and playing instruments) and having a good time doing it.

Five | The Welcome Song

The welcome song sets the tone for the entire session. If it is done effectively, participants will be energized and ready to "tackle" whatever additional activities you have planned. The therapist should always arrive early enough to get the room set up, to have conversations with those who have already arrived, and to demonstrate an attitude of genuine caring for the individuals. This attitude is something that should come naturally for a person who has chosen music therapy as a career, but we can all improve our skills in this area.

PURPOSE OF THE WELCOME SONG

The purpose of a welcome song is just that—a way to begin the session with music in a way that is non-threatening and "fun" for the participants. It can be—and should be—much more than that. In the nursing home environment people from all different backgrounds are thrown together much against their wills, and the effects of being a part of this new block of humanity can be extremely frustrating and even debilitating. If these "strangers" can in some way get to know one another as fellow human beings, the chances for maintaining quality of life are greatly enhanced.

The purpose of this chapter is to present some musical ideas for welcoming individuals (whether new to the group or those returning) with at least three goals in mind:

1. Getting them to participate in the music making by singing and/or rhythmic movements.

2. Getting them to learn one another's names.

3. Getting them to immediately feel the good things that music can do for their present mood.

STRUCTURE OF THE WELCOME SONG

As stated previously, I remember trying to present a new welcome song at every session. Everyone in the group enjoyed these, because I am a good songwriter; however, I realized one day that the session and the song are not about me. I am not here to perform and receive recognition for that performance. I am here to create an environment in which all members of the group are the performers, and I am just the facilitator.

Some of my efforts actually leaned toward that outcome, but it took me a while to realize what was happening. The following song is an example of a moment that was moving in the right direction. Eventually I realized that this was the way to go.

Big Cheer Song

> *Cindy is here to make music.*
> *Cindy is here to make music.*
> *Cindy is here. Let's give her a great big cheer. (WHEEE!)*
> *Cindy—we're glad you're here.*

> *[Joseph Pinson © 2005]*

Originally the lyric of the song was strict AABA form:

> *Cindy is here to make music.*
> *Cindy is here to make music.*
> *Cindy is here. Cindy is here.*
> *Cindy is here to make music.*

Since the "B" section is really just a repetition of elements of the "A" section, the song was really AAAA (the *most* accessible lyric form). One of the members of the group suggested "Let's give her a great big cheer," and suddenly we had a song in which everyone could participate with "WHEEE" or whatever sound they chose to contribute.

Even though the song was quite simple, I distinctly remember not encouraging everyone to sing, because I still looked upon it as *my* welcome song. Whenever I use this song in my current practice, I not only encourage everyone to sing every time, but I also add some extra "stuff" to keep the rhythm going. It has evolved to the following.

We're Glad You're Here

Cindy is here to make music. (clap-clap-clap)
Cindy is here to make music. (clap-clap-clap)
Cindy is here. Let's give her a great big cheer. (WHEEE!)
Cindy, (clap-clap-clap) we're glad you're here. (clap-clap-clap)

[Joseph Pinson © 2012]

The idea of making persons feel welcome in the group is a good one. It seems to be a recurring theme with me. The song below had the hand clapping from the beginning, but the words in the middle section were more complicated. Below is the version that I would recommend for seniors.

We're So Glad You're Here

Billy (clap-clap), Billy (clap-clap), we're so glad you're here today.
Billy (clap-clap), Billy (clap-clap), we're so glad you're here today.
We're so glad you're here—to help us sing and play.
Billy (clap-clap), Billy (clap-clap), we're so glad you're here today.

[Joseph Pinson © 2012]

All of this hand clapping is probably something that some seniors don't enjoy, because of sensitive skin or other pain that might come with this sort of activity. Although I have not tried this to date, I may begin using claves for the songs that involve clapping.

ACCOMPANIED OR UNACCOMPANIED

Most of the time I use live accompaniment (keyboard or guitar) with the two preceding songs; however, either or both of them could be done a cappella. I still have a personal preference for the accompaniment, but my preferences are changing in favor of what works best to get a good response from the clientele. Occasionally you will have one of the members of a senior group who plays the piano or guitar. It is good to let them use their skills in this way, but probably not during every session. It is also possible to create accompaniment with hand-held chimes, with three members of the group each holding two chimes that represent a chord (the first and third of the chords needed). The therapist can point to each person as the chord is needed in the song. The following song was designed for unaccompanied voice.

Basic Hello Song #1

Hello! (clap-clap) Hello! (clap-clap) George is here. (clap-clap-clap)
Hello! (clap-clap) Hello! (clap-clap) George is here. (clap-clap-clap)
Hello! Hello! Hello! Hello! George is here. (clap-clap-clap)

[Joseph Pinson © 2012]

You will note that it has only three phrases instead of four, but it works very nicely. The four consecutive "hello"s help to keep participants focused on the basic message of the song. It should be presented in the same key at each session, because someone with perfect pitch or very good sensitivity to pitch would be more encouraged to sing. I wrote another similar song for two reasons:

1. To offer the reader some variety.

2. To fill the half page under the first basic hello in the Appendix.

Basic Hello Song #2

Hello Sandra! (clap-clap-clap) Hello Sandra! (clap-clap-clap)
Hello Sandra! (clap-clap-clap) Hello Sandra! (clap-clap-clap)
We're so glad, so glad, so glad you're here today. (clap-clap-clap)

[Joseph Pinson © 2012]

In the time before this information was published I was using a very simple greeting song that included no motor movement. It seemed to work pretty well, and I am thinking that there may be situations where it is more appropriate than the ones with clapping. One could say that the opening song is a good time to "wake up and participate"; however, if we take the Iso-Principle into consideration, there are certainly times when the mood of the group is one that the therapist should approach with something much less demanding. Certainly, singing should be encouraged, but nothing more, if a mood change is in order.

Greeting Song

Hello Cynthia, hello Cynthia. We're glad you're here today.
Hello Cynthia, hello Cynthia. We're glad you're here today.

[Joseph Pinson © 2012]

This song is much shorter than the others—asking for much less from participants. In the version that appears in the Appendix I have added two variations—one with two handbells or hand-held chimes and the other with rhythmic clapping (or claves). These additions would probably be made after the group becomes familiar with the song.

In the version with bells or chimes one or two (octave) would be given to each person as his/her name is sung. The individual responds with the instruments when cued by the therapist.

The version with clapping or claves may be best presented without accompaniment, if the therapist is working alone. In this way he/she can lead the singing and give visual cues for the clapping or claves. All three versions are included in the Appendix.

PRESENTATION OF THE OPENING SONG

Once the therapist has chosen a song for opening, I recommend that this same song be used for the entire treatment period. In the academic setting this would be the semester. If the therapist serves a facility throughout the year, I would recommend at least a quarterly period of use before a new song is introduced. The rationale for keeping the same song for several sessions is to allow everyone the opportunity to really learn the song. Someone may say, "The song is *so* simple— why would they need more time to learn it?" Within every group of seniors there are some with more advanced stages of dementia who will have difficulty accessing even the simplest material. Repetition may be the key to getting them involved.

If this were the only song that we used every week, there would be no argument against change and variation, but this is only the opener. Every session contains other opportunities for the introduction of new musical material where other skills are measured. There are at least three other arguments for using the same song:

1. Some persons in the group will not immediately remember that they have sung this song before; in fact, some will not remember that they sang it just a moment ago.

2. It represents a stable, predictable first step into the world of music therapy for those who do remember.

3. Those who already know the song will take pride in helping others learn the song.

It is also possible the same song may be used each week with the gradual introduction of new material (bells or chimes or clapping) as in the "Greeting Song" stated previously.

Be sure that whatever song you use is in a range that is easily sung. It should be a range that is close to that of conversation. For most persons this is the C scale in treble for women and in bass clef for men. The most accessible songs have a range of less than an octave. The greatest hit of all times in the special needs camp is "He's Got the Whole World in His Hands" (range of a sixth *plus* a lyric form A-A-A-A). Seniors are persons with special needs. Don't forget that.

Step one

Be sure that your group is set up in a semicircle facing you, the therapist, in order that you can make eye contact with everyone. If they can be close enough to one another to allow shaking hands and passing instruments, that is good; however, this is not always possible because of the size of some wheelchairs and the presence of recliners, scooters, etc. To have the group face a wall or a window is better than their facing the open hallway where others pass. No space is ideal, unless you have the luxury of a music therapy room.

Step two

After a friendly verbal welcome to music therapy, tell everyone present that we begin with an opening song. Invite those who already know the song to sing with you. Since the song contains a name, use your own. Yes, in sense you are welcoming yourself to the session, and although that may seem unusual, you should remember that "unusual" usually translates to "fun" in a session, and if we're not having fun, we should be doing something else. If you are reading this and thinking, "Who is this person, and why is he telling me this?" I am an old guy with 35 years' experience who knows that having fun is a *principal* ingredient in music therapy that is effective.

Step three

After naming yourself ("I'm Joe"), move to the left or to the right in the circle. If you know that person from a previous session, say "And this is Susan" (assuming that is her name). If you are just meeting that person, say, "And what is your name?" If you have met the person before but don't remember his/her name, say, "I know you have been here before, but I am having trouble remembering your name. Please remind me." With this kind of statement, you have let the group know two important things:

1. You are honest.

2. You also have trouble remembering names at times. They love to know that someone else also has difficulty in this area.

Step four

When you have a name for that person, remind everyone that it is time to sing by saying, "Let's all sing to (name of person)." Begin the singing with a verbal indicator of tempo, such as "Ready, sing" or "Here we go." Do not *count*. This is not a band or a choir. This is a group of seniors—many of whom know nothing about music. Step four must be repeated with the greeting of each person to remind participants that it is time to sing again, to remind them that you are not here to sing for them, and to remind them that you *expect* them to sing.

Step five

Continue by saying, "Let's review. My name (pointing to yourself) is _____." Let them fill in the blank. If no one in the group remembers, remind them. Move attention to the person to whom you have just sung and say, "And this is _____." Let the group fill in the blank. If they don't remember, remind them. Sing the song again—reminding them that it is time to sing. I tell the members of my jazz band that the hardest thing for me is not remembering the words—but remembering when to sing.

Step six

Move attention to the next person in the group. As soon as you have a name, repeat the process in Step Four. After singing to that person, repeat the "review" process in Step five. This process continues until all members of the group have been named and welcomed. This may take a few minutes to complete, but the end result is well worth the time spent.

What is happening here? The therapist is engaging the members of the group in welcoming each person through the medium of music that will help each person remember names. The therapist is reinforcing his/her knowledge in the process. Persons in the group are learning the names of folks that they see every day. It might just be the start of a friendship.

If participants are close enough to shake the hand of the persons on either side of them, and if time permits, you might consider adding this song at the conclusion of the activity. It would be led by the therapist without encouraging singing in order to get full participation.

Shake Hands

Shake hands. (shake-shake) Shake hands. (shake-shake)
Shake hands with the person on your right.
When you shake say "How are you?" It's a friendly thing to do.

[Joseph Pinson, ASCAP © 2012]

The therapist would be at the end of the semicircle where the individual had no one to his/her right. At the conclusion of this first statement, move to the other end of the group and sing:

> *Shake hands. (shake-shake) Shake hands. (shake-shake)*
> *Shake hands with the person on your left.*
> *When you shake say "How are you?" It's a friendly thing to do.*

If there is an aide or student helper present, that person may go to the end of the line as needed. This would allow the therapist the option of doing the song with accompaniment, if desired.

There will be situations regarding the total time of the session that may get in the way of using this song, but if the group or an individual in the group has an objective regarding shaking hands, this is a good song for addressing that task.

SUMMARY OF CHAPTER 5

The welcome song sets the tone for the entire session. If it is done effectively, participants will be energized and ready to "tackle" whatever additional activities you have planned.

The purpose of a welcome song is just that—a way to begin the session with music in a way that is non-threatening and "fun" for the participants. If these "strangers" can in some way get to know one another as fellow human beings, the chances for maintaining quality of life are greatly enhanced. The strategies include:

1. Getting them to participate in the music making by singing and/or rhythmic movements.

2. Getting them to learn one another's names.

3. Getting them to immediately feel the good things that music can do for their present mood.

As stated previously, I remember trying to present a new welcome song at every session. Everyone in the group enjoyed these, because I am a good songwriter; however, I realized one day that the session and the song are not about me. Even though the songs were quite simple, I distinctly remember not encouraging everyone to sing, because I still looked upon it as *my* welcome song. During the songs that I use today I encourage everyone to sing every time, and I also add some extra "stuff" (handclapping, chimes, movement) to keep the rhythm going.

Most of the time I use live accompaniment (keyboard or guitar) with the songs; however, most of them could be done a cappella. Occasionally you will have one of the members of a senior group who plays the piano or guitar. It is good to let them use their skills in this way, but probably not during every session. It is also possible to create accompaniment with hand-held chimes cued by the therapist.

Once the therapist has chosen a song for opening, I recommend that this same song be used for the entire treatment period. In the academic setting this would be the semester. The rationale for keeping the same song for several sessions is to allow everyone the opportunity to really learn the song.

There are six steps that I have found effective for presentation of the welcome song:

1. Be sure that your group is set up in a semicircle facing you, the therapist, in order that you can make eye contact with everyone.

2. After a friendly verbal welcome to music therapy, tell everyone present that we begin with an opening song. Invite those who already know the song to sing with you. Use your own name for the first rendition.

3. After naming yourself ("I'm _____"), move to the left or to the right in the circle. "And now we will sing to _____." If the person is new or you don't remember the name, ask. Seniors really appreciate honesty.

4. When you have a name for that person, remind everyone that it is time to sing by saying, "Let's all sing to _____." Every time you sing the song you must remind participants that it is time to sing again.

5. Review each name that has been sung. Give seniors an opportunity to be part of this process.

6. Move attention to the next person in the group. As soon as you have a name, ask everyone to sing to that person. Continue until all members of the group have been named and welcomed. This may take a few minutes to complete, but the end result is well worth the time spent.

Six | *Structured Motor Strategy*

Even persons with no training in music can pass out rhythm instruments, set a beat (either by playing a leading instrument such as claves or go-go bells or by playing a rhythmic CD), and invite everyone to join in the fun. This is certainly better than no motor strategy, but it falls far short in comparison to that which a trained music therapist can provide.

At one time I thought that since I was providing live accompaniment with the option of varying the tempo or the style, this was certainly more than adequate. I was wrong. This strategy should be designed to engage the participants in a meaningful set of exercises that stimulates their imagination and holds their interest for at least five minutes—and sometimes longer.

PURPOSE OF THE MOTOR STRATEGY

For a motor strategy to have a positive impact on participants, the therapist should plan something that engages as many skills as possible. Playing instruments is good, but playing *and* singing is so much better.

Done properly the motor strategy should involve motor skills, cognitive skills and communication skills, because the more of these we can get participants to do simultaneously, the better the exercise for the brain. It is more than just movement. It is a multi-tasking regimen that with regular use will keep them healthy longer.

For this strategy to be effective the therapist must use simple melodies that are easy to sing in a range that is comfortable. Incorporating variations beyond the basic "let's all play" section requires that the individuals listen and respond appropriately. The structure of the music makes this much easier than following random directions.

STRUCTURE OF THE MOTOR STRATEGY

The music therapist must find a familiar song that most seniors have encountered somewhere along the way. The song should be simple enough that even younger persons (whom we see fairly often in nursing homes) will be able to access it without much difficulty. A lot of these tunes are in my 74-year-old memory bank, but when I am looking for new ideas, I go to the website of the Public Domain Information Project, better known as PD INFO (www.pdinfo.com). Here you will find lists of hundreds of older songs in different categories (popular songs, patriotic songs, Christian hymns, spirituals, Christmas songs, and children's songs)—and yes, we use children's songs with seniors, if the words are appropriate, or if they can be adapted to fit the older crowd.

At the moment of writing this paragraph I went to the site and found an old tune that I had not sung nor thought of in many years. It is called "Old Grey Mare." It is not only a song that will work for our purposes of rhythmic variation, but it is also one about which many seniors would say, "That is *my* song—a great description of who I am." If you are not familiar with the melody, you can find it on YouTube. Here are the words.

Old Grey Mare

> *The old grey mare she ain't what she used to be,*
> *ain't what she used to be, ain't what she used to be.*
> *The old grey mare she ain't what she used to be*
> *many long years ago.*
>
> *REFRAIN: Many long years ago. Many long years ago.*
> *The old grey mare she ain't what she used to be*
> *many long years ago.*
>
> *[traditional, 1918]*

It is a perfect song for our purposes—a simple, straightforward idea with lots of repetition of lyrics and melody. After finding a song that seems to fit the criteria that I have in mind, I begin to think about ways to create a rhythmic variation. This one practically writes itself. In the variation below the claps are for the music therapist (as leader). They also represent the moments that the group plays their rhythm instruments:

> *The old grey mare (clap-clap-clap)*
> *she ain't what she used to be, (clap-clap-clap)*
> *ain't what she used to be, (clap-clap-clap)*
> *ain't what she used to be. (clap-clap-clap)*

The old gray mare (clap-clap-clap)

she ain't what she used to be (clap-clap-clap)

many long years ago. (clap-clap-clap)

Many long years ago. (clap-clap-clap)

Many long years ago. (clap-clap-clap)

The old grey mare (clap-clap-clap)

she ain't what she used to be (clap-clap-clap)

many long years ago. (clap-clap-clap)

My former student, Brett Koltuniak, developed a second variation that has been very popular with the seniors. He sings phrases of the song with a hold (fermata) on certain words (usually the last in the phrase—but not always). At this point the participants shake their instruments as long as the leader holds the note. The leader pauses briefly before continuing to the next phrase. The unpredictability of this variation means that everyone has to watch the director to know when to play—and they love every minute of it.

PRESENTATION OF THE MOTOR STRATEGY

For the motor strategy to be effective it is important have some control over:

1. the number of persons in the group

2. the environmental arrangement of the group

3. facilitating physical assistance, if needed.

For this strategy to be delivered effectively there should be no more than eight persons in the group. Six is ideal. Ten is workable, but a stretch. The participants should be in a semicircle facing the therapist—as close as possible to one another. If someone in the group needs physical assistance to participate, a helper can be very useful. There is also some advantage to having the members of the group help one another. One member can hold a clave while it is struck by someone who has use of only one hand.

Step one

Give a hand-held rhythm instrument to each participant.

All members may receive the same instrument, or you may split the group (four maracas and four woodblocks). If the latter are used, have all of the maraca players side by side and the same for the wood blockers. If you ask for one of these to play, they will be in a "section" that helps them know when to respond. Give directions on how to hold and play each instrument. Present the tune that you have chosen (usually just the refrain), and encourage everyone to play the instruments. At the conclusion of that first rendition, say, "Now that you know the song, I want you to play *and* sing." Accompaniment is useful here, but not an absolute necessity. Do not give instructions about the rhythm patterns used in the song. Just say, "Everyone play and sing." Sometimes it is useful to set a verbal tempo by saying, "Ready—Go." Here is a song that seniors enjoy.

Moonlight Bay

We were sailing along—on Moonlight Bay
We could hear the voices ringing. They seemed to say
"You have stolen my heart". "Now don't go 'way".
As we sang love's old sweet song on Moonlight Bay.

[Weinrich and Madden, 1918]

At the end of this introductory version compliment everyone for their playing. Do it a second time, and encourage more singing *and* playing.

Step two

Introduce the first variation. This is probably best done without accompaniment in order that you will have hands free to lead the responses. Instruct the participants to play their instruments when you clap your hands. Remind them to help you sing. A useful verbal count-off is "Ready—Sing" (in tempo).

We were sailing along (clap-clap-clap-clap)
on Moonlight Bay (clap-clap-clap-clap)
We could hear the voices ringing (clap-clap-clap)
They seemed to say (clap-clap-clap-clap)
"You have stolen my heart" (clap-clap-clap-clap)
"Now don't go 'way" (clap-clap-clap-clap)
As we sang love's old sweet song
on Moonlight Bay (clap-clap-clap)

Is this simple? YES. Is it boring? NO—not for the seniors. How many therapists go to this second step? Not many. Compliment the members of the group, and ask them to do it again. Encourage more singing *and* playing.

Step three

In this variation say, "I will sing, and you play your instruments when I hold a note." In this version the held notes can come at any place in the melody. The last word in the phrase is a good place to start. In the version "**bold**" means "**hold**." Pause after each hold, and make the group listen for the next part. The tempo should be a little slower on this version.

> *We were sailing* **along**—*on Moonlight* **Bay**
> *We could* **hear** *the voices ringing. They seemed to* **say**
> *"You have stolen my* **heart**.*" "Now don't* **go** *'way."*
> *As we sang love's old sweet* **song** *on Moonlight* **Bay**.

They will enjoy this enough that you will probably want to repeat it, with holds coming at different places.

Step four

Go back to the first version. Encourage everyone to play *and* sing. Repeat it one more time at a faster tempo. If you are using accompaniment, you might want to move to a higher key. At the end repeat the last phrase and augment it (make it longer) with the last few notes as a big finale. They will follow.

> *As we sang love's old sweet song*
> *on Moon —— light —— Bay ———.*

This is a rhythmic *workout*—not just "instrument play." This song is a little more complex than "Old Grey Mare," but most seniors know it, and even some with a severe impairment of cognition may be able to sing it.

I am not including many written variations in this work, because, now that you know the technique, you can begin to make these up for yourself.

Here is a small list of other possible tunes that may be used in this way: "Battle Hymn" (refrain), "Bill Bailey," "By the Light of the Silvery Moon," "Camptown Races," "In My Merry Oldsmobile," "Ja-Da," "Let Me Call You Sweetheart," "Put on Your Old Grey Bonnet," "Shine on Harvest Moon," "Skip to My Lou," "Take Me Out to the Ball Game," "This Land Is Your Land," "When the Saints Go Marching in," "When You're Smilin'," "You're a Grand Old Flag."

One word of caution (from experience): Songs in triple meter (3/4 time) do not lend themselves to the variations with clapping. In the list above these are: "In My Merry Oldsmobile," "Let Me Call You Sweetheart" and "Take Me Out to the Ball Game." For this purpose you will have to convert them to duple meter. I have included sample conversions of these songs in the Appendix to give you a better idea about what is required.

SUMMARY OF CHAPTER 6

Even persons with no training in music can pass out rhythm instruments, set a beat, and invite everyone to join in the fun. This is not enough. This strategy should be designed to engage the participants in a meaningful set of exercises that stimulates their imagination and holds their interest for at least five minutes—and sometimes longer.

Playing instruments is good, but playing *and* singing is so much better. Done properly the motor strategy should involve motor skills, cognitive skills, and communication skills, because the more of these we can get participants to do simultaneously, the better the exercise for the brain.

The music therapist must find a familiar song that most seniors have encountered somewhere along the way. The song should be simple enough that even younger persons (whom we see fairly often in nursing homes) will be able to access it without much difficulty.

For the motor strategy to be effective it is important have some control over the number of persons in the group, the environmental arrangement of the group, and facilitating physical assistance, if needed. For this strategy to be delivered effectively there should be no more than eight persons in the group. Six is ideal.

Presentation of the motor strategy is divided into four parts:

1. Give a hand-held rhythm instrument to each participant. Give directions on how to hold and play each instrument. Present the tune that you have chosen, and encourage everyone to play the instruments. At the conclusion of that first rendition say, "Now that you know the song, I want you to play *and* sing."

2. Introduce the first variation with rhythmic insertions. This is probably best done without accompaniment in order that you will have hands free to lead the responses. Instruct the participants to play their instruments when you clap your hands.

3. For the second variation say, "I will sing, and you play your instruments when I hold a note." In this version the held notes can come at any place in the melody. Pause after each hold, and make the group listen for the next part.

4. Go back to the first version. Encourage everyone to play and sing. Repeat it one more time at a faster tempo. If you are using accompaniment, you might want to move to a higher key. At the end repeat the last phrase and augment it (make it longer) with the last few notes as big finale. They will follow.

Seven | *The Question/ Answer Song*

RATIONALE FOR THE SONG

Seniors in assisted living or nursing homes have many things in common. They are isolated from friends and family either by choice (theirs or that of another), by dementia that renders them incapable of making reasonable choices, or by other barriers of physical and/or mental deterioration. This isolation contributes to problems such as depression, anxiety, difficulty in communication, helplessness, loss of motivation, loss of appetite, loneliness, sleeplessness, memory loss, and many others. Any strategy by anyone (family, friends, caregivers, therapists) that can lift them from this state—even for a short period of time—is a very worthwhile endeavor. Music therapists are uniquely gifted to offer a real time (here and now) experience that can address many of these problems in the moment and in many instances have a lasting effect upon the quality of life for these individuals. To achieve this objective we must understand that it is our job to engage seniors in music making—in spite of their physical and mental condition, in spite of the distractions that may be present, and in spite of the fact that this requires careful planning and delivery of our services.

PURPOSES OF THE SONG

The purposes of the question/answer song include the following:

1. To encourage seniors to discuss elements of their lives, past and present.

2. To assist them in forming bonds of interest and support within the group based upon shared or similar experiences.

3. To encourage their playing instruments *and* singing a user-friendly song that relates to a common interest. Most of us have observed seniors remembering the words to songs from their youth—even though these words may have little or no meaning for them. It is quite another thing to see them recall experiences from days gone that they can describe in some way to other members of their "family," which is what the institutional community has become, whether they realize it or not. Since socialization is always one of the goals in groups of this type, what could be more "social" than telling your stories to those persons who are part of your immediate "family"?

ORIGIN OF THE SONG

I don't remember ever observing another therapist using the question/answer song, nor do I claim to be the originator. My work with seniors has evolved from a time that I served younger and middle-aged persons with developmental disabilities in a residential facility. Their responses were similar to what I see in the senior population, but their cognition and life experience were quite different. The individuals whom I see in nursing homes and similar facilities have in many instances been reduced to a name on a chart (if they have allowed it), but they were once productive members of society. They have wonderful stories to tell, if we can provide a musical framework to allow this kind of expression.

Neither do I remember the exact time that I began using this strategy, but that is not important. It is good for one who aspires to work with the senior population to acknowledge things one doesn't remember. It is also good in all therapeutic encounters to understand that, regardless of the clientele, we are more alike than different. This attitude paves the way for creation of a "common ground of sound" (Pinson, 1989) that is essential for success—ours and theirs. It is easy for me to say this, because at age 74 I am definitely one of them, whether I want to admit it or not. For younger people to make this connection may be a little more difficult, but they have the advantage of being able to offer the seniors a glimpse of what they used to be, and if this relationship is handled appropriately, both the young music therapist and the persons served will receive great benefit.

Some of the first songs of this type that I used in my practice employed questions that required a simple answer, e.g., "Who is your favorite president?" or "Who is your favorite movie star?" I was surprised that answers for these questions were quite difficult for some of the participants, because in general they seemed to be pretty alert. In this respect they are also like the adults with developmental disabilities whom I once served. On the surface many appear to be normal. It is not until you start asking questions that their cognitive deficits become apparent.

Answers to the initial questions could be expanded by adding "And why did you like Ronald Reagan?" The women would usually reply, "Because he was a good-looking man." When I asked, "What was your favorite John Wayne movie?" most persons had no answer. In retrospect I realize that these questions, although very basic and general, were somewhat like a mini-history exam that dealt with second-hand information that was not a part of the real life experience of the participants. Yes, they had seen Ronald Reagan on television and John Wayne in movies, but that is not the same as knowing these persons in real life. Studies have shown that music is useful in assisting persons with recall of certain memories, such as the words and/or melody of a song or events from their lives; however, this recall does not usually extend to facts of history or other academic subjects.

On one occasion I asked the seniors to name the first president that they remember. My own response would have been "Franklin Roosevelt," and, since most of them had a few years on me, I expected to hear names that predated FDR. Instead they named persons who had been in office since the advent of television. It was obvious that these visual images had helped keep some of these names in their banks of memories. Let me digress to say that the visual memory may be the first to go when cognitive skills begin to deteriorate. When I would visit my late aunt in her last years, she did not recognize me, although her vision was still pretty good. As soon as I called her name, she knew who I was by the sound of my voice.

With these early explorations I would try to personalize the song, i.e., "My favorite movie star is—John Wayne. My favorite movie star is—John Wayne. He is the best on the big silver screen. My favorite movie star is—John Wayne." It is a "dumb" song (a very dumb song), but what made it even worse was the fact that, since it was personalized for an individual, my encouraging everyone in the group to sing was a request that made no sense whatsoever. At the time I didn't seem to mind that everyone would not sing, because I was content to be in what I would describe as a "quasi-performance" mode. The seniors in my group seemed to enjoy the old songs that I brought them every week, and if my popularity had been rated at the time, I would have received very good marks. Unfortunately, I was surely overlooking some of the wonderful derivatives that can occur when one makes music therapy the primary focus, while saving the "dog and pony show" for another audience.

I think that a lot of persons in the music therapy field have a need to perform, and certainly, if we are not comfortable in that role, we will have some difficulty doing what we need to do. My students participate in a local "open mic" each semester as part of their training. It has little or nothing to do with music therapy, but if they are not able to find some success with that type of audience, then their developing the skills needed to be competent in our field may be in question. As music therapists we need to realize that our performance must always be secondary to providing a framework for the therapeutic process; otherwise, we will not be able to provide services that are effective. Furthermore, once we learn to get beyond performance, we must constantly *remind* seniors (and remind ourselves) that we are there only to help *them* make music.

A NEW DIRECTION

There was a breakthrough that occurred somewhat by accident. One of the group members asked permission to tell a story. He told about a sign that had been placed on the bulletin board in the facility that said "HAVE A GREAT DAY." Later on someone crossed through the word "HAVE" and inserted "MAKE." What a great story—what a great message. I was able to improvise the following song. It is very accessible, and it was certainly one that I could encourage everyone to sing.

Make a Great Day

> *You've got to make—make a great day.*
> *You've got to make—make a great day.*
> *In everything you do and say,*
> *you've got to make—make a great day.*

[Joseph Pinson © 2012]

The simplicity of the lyric is critical for the success of this strategy. The common fault of most writers, even professionals, is to try to include too many words. This may have started with something like "You've got to do everything you can—to make this a very good day." WRONG! You can set these words to music, but it is just too much. We are not on Broadway—we're in the Broadway Nursing Home. This version also leaves out the critical line (from the gentleman who told the story) "Make a great day." In this song the "B" section rhymes, but this was not necessary. I could have said "Find something you can do for others,'" and the song would still achieve its purpose. Certainly the rhyme helps in retaining the lyric, but it is not required. This is probably not the best example, because this song practically wrote itself—on the spot. We will discuss more about lyric writing in another chapter.

With each statement of the song I encouraged the members of the group to sing, and they did. This reminder is very important, because in some cases an individual may not remember his/her name, what day it is, that he/she is supposed to sing, or that he/she sang the same song just a few minutes before.

The question for each person in the group was, "What will you do to help make it a great day?" An answer requires some creative forethought that is usually expressed in more than one word. Responses included things like "I'm going to smile," "I'm going to be a better friend," "I'm going to read my Bible," and the one that brought the house down, "I'm going to mind my own business." That was from Sandra, the class clown. Nearly every senior group has one. I don't know whether they plan their antics or whether it just comes out. When you discover who this person is, you can begin to depend on him/her to interpret the present moment (with humor), critique your singing (with humor), remind you that you need a haircut (with humor), and/or just give you an occasional look and a smile that will inspire you to do better things—in the moment and in the future.

This song speaks to the *present* circumstances of the participants and is, in my opinion, much more relevant for effective therapy than what I had done before. We need to always be on the lookout for strategies that will improve the lives of those we serve in the environment in which they find themselves at the moment. This is their home. This is their life. This is who they are. When seniors can accept this and learn to live as fully as possible in their new home, the problems become less for them, and their positive attitude helps others who may be struggling.

At the time that the "Great Day" song was written I did not have the "light bulb moment" that told me to shift my songwriting in this direction, but after a few more weeks the part of my brain that unconsciously analyzes things began to show me what was needed. If your mind tells you that "I haven't seen this in the literature" or "We have always done it this way," then you are not being open to the creative potential that is in all of us. The brain, being the powerful force that it is, also eventually led me to redesign the greeting, the motor strategy, and the closing.

The new direction of which I speak is one in which individuals are encouraged to process and discuss real experiences from their own lives instead of those things that are second hand, such as presidents and movie stars. The therapist begins to focus on the individual: who they are, what they have done, where they have been, and what they believe. One that I have found very successful is this one.

There's Something about Me

There's something about me that you don't know.
There's something about me that you don't know.
There's something you don't know, and I swear it's really so.
There's something about me that you don't know.

[Joseph Pinson © 2012]

The lyric can be learned by most persons after the first hearing, and the melody that I used (see the Appendix) is simple and easy to sing. Note that the form of the lyric is the same as the one before (**A A B A**), which means that the participants are really only learning two lines (A and B). This is another instance where rhyme is not necessary in the "B" section, but its presence surely helps. In this one there is internal rhyme within the line ("There's something you don't *know*, and I swear it's really *so*.") that makes it even easier to remember.

Each participant is asked to tell the group something positive about himself/herself. One woman told about her experience as a music teacher. A man told about the Chevrolet pick-up that he owned when he was a teenager. A few had nothing to offer (taking the Fifth Amendment), but in general the rate of participation was very high. I began by telling them that I had been married four times and lived on four continents. It was a gross exaggeration but got a good laugh, and, as we will discuss further in other chapters, laughter is a very important part of what we do. I tell students that if they can't learn to laugh at themselves, they are training for the wrong profession. When we can learn to laugh at our own problems while leading a group, the members begin to understand that this is an acceptable practice that they might find useful for themselves.

PRESENTATION OF THE SONG

Step one

Each person is given a set of claves. Before I purchased the claves, we used rhythm sticks. During one session a woman complained that these are "children's instruments." I responded by saying that she was correct. I pointed out that there is an adult version of these called "claves." They are made of rosewood and cost about 25 dollars a pair. I suggested that I would be more than happy to use these, if someone in the group wanted to purchase a set. End of discussion—but not the end of the story. We are now using claves. I found a way to purchase these, and to date we have been very happy with the responses. I don't think the change was actually necessary, but, in fact, the claves sound much better and are probably easier to hold because of their thickness. Listening to the comments and requests of those we serve is a very useful trait for music therapists. Having an instrument that requires two hands to play is important for total involvement. You will encounter persons who can only use one hand because of a stroke or other disability. Most of these persons have already devised a method for doing things that usually requires two hands, so we see them holding one clave between the legs or in the armpit. They may also tap one or both sticks on the arm of a wheelchair. To allow each person the opportunity to adapt in whatever way is most comfortable is reinforcing to acceptance of the present situation. If someone does need assistance, we can provide that, or, more importantly, we can let them assist one another. If you and your neighbor can share something like playing claves, this may well pave the way for future conversations and even friendship. The musical environment creates a situation in which sharing responsibilities is not unusual or threatening.

I remember working with an individual who was very intimidated by touch of any kind (tactile defensiveness). I accepted her condition and designed strategies where touch was not important or perhaps even unnecessary. One day we were playing "boomwhackers" face to face, and on sudden impulse I touched one of her instruments with one of mine. She smiled the biggest smile that I had ever seen, and began initiating touch in this way herself. Music had allowed her a type of social contact that she had never been able to accept previously.

Step two

The question/answer song is presented one time by the therapist, and then everyone is encouraged to sing and play the claves. A "special instrument" (a hand-held that can be heard above the sound of the claves) is given to the person whose turn it is to answer the question. Occasionally I will bring a suspended cymbal or roto-tom and place it in front of the person.

The use of rhythm instruments accomplishes these things:

1. Playing the claves gives everyone something to do while the focus is upon the person who has just answered the question.

2. Playing the claves improves the level of attention and participation in singing.

3. Passing the special instrument helps the group focus on the person who is answering the question.

4. The special instrument allows each individual a time to be recognized by the group—whether they play with gusto or in a very subdued manner. With each rendition of the song participants are reminded to sing and play their instruments. The special instrument is always passed from left to right or vice-versa. This allows everyone to see that no one is being left out and also provides the opportunity for one individual to pass the instrument to the next, when that is possible.

MORE IDEAS FOR SONGS

Holidays and special seasons can provide ideas for songs that bring back personal memories. Try to avoid those questions that don't demand much creativity for an answer—things like, "What is your favorite food at Thanksgiving?" or "What is your favorite Christmas song?" I guess the latter is okay, if you are prepared to sing (on the spot) part of each song mentioned (time consuming), but it still does not require much cognitive ability from the participant. One song in this category that set the stage for some very excellent participation was this one.

I Remember Halloween Long Ago

I remember Halloween long ago.
I remember Halloween long ago.
All the things we did when I was just a kid.
I remember Halloween long ago.

[Joseph Pinson © 2012]

Note that I have used the same lyric form again (**A A B A**). Does anyone get tired of this? Maybe you do, but the seniors you serve who are struggling to manage information will find it very reassuring. **A A B A** is part of our musical DNA, because a large part of the music that we have experienced in our lifetimes uses that form. The simple form makes the song easier to remember and, probably, easier to sing. On one occasion when I presented this song, I learned from the seniors that, once upon a time, before you could purchase a costume at the local drugstore, boys used to dress as girls, and girls would also cross this boundary. In the minds of many it is no longer politically correct, but I was surprised that preceding generations thought nothing of it as a costume alternative for Halloween.

Since beginning to offer songs that tapped into the personal experience of the participants I have used one that is a little more complicated, but for some reason the level of participation has been very good. Perhaps it is because it speaks strongly to the daily challenges of living in the institution. It uses call and response in which the therapist sings a line—followed by a response from the group. The last two lines are sung by everyone. These are the words. The group responses are in parentheses.

I Expect Respect

I don't care (I don't care) who you are, (who you are,)
or where you're from, (or where you're from,)
or what you do. (or what you do.)
This is what I expect—I expect respect.
I expect respect from you.

[Joseph Pinson © 2012]

This chant is obviously more than **A A B A**, but it works nicely, because of the call and response section at the beginning. In presenting it to the group I found that the most effective accompaniment was an African drum. The question was, "Do you get a lot of respect?"—to which most answered "No!" The second question was, "What do you think you could do as an individual to get more respect?" Most agreed that showing respect for others (especially the staff) was the best way to improve one's own chances of receiving the same.

Another useful lyric form for the question/answer song is **A A A B**. In the example that I offer, the "B" section rhymes with the "A"s. It is nice but not necessary. Once you have stated the "A" three times, the listener doesn't notice that the concluding phrase does not rhyme. Another feature of this song is that I have used a familiar tune (actually a children's song) that most seniors remember. A tune that they recognize improves the possibility for greater participation. The words are as follows.

This is What I Do

(to the tune of "This Little Light of Mine", 1920)

> *This is what I do—when I'm feeling blue.*
> *This is what I do—when I'm feeling blue.*
> *This is what I do—when I'm feeling blue.*
> *It works for me. It just might work for you.*

A song about "being blue" is near and dear to the hearts of seniors in nursing homes. They know exactly what we are singing about. The song brings to them the added dimension of learning that everyone in the group has good days and bad days, and they learn about how to deal with this feeling from other members of the group.

SUMMARY OF CHAPTER 7

Remember that the purposes of the question/answer song include the following:

1. To encourage seniors to discuss elements of their lives, past and present (because their lives are rich in experience).

2. To assist them in forming bonds of interest and support within the group based upon shared or similar experiences (because telling stories is a wonderful way to get to know one another).

3. To encourage their playing instruments and singing a user-friendly song that relates to a common interest. Most of the seniors in our groups have at one time participated in singing. Maybe they stopped because of lack of interest or because someone told them they "couldn't carry a tune in a bucket." It is the job of the music therapist to reignite that interest, because making music in this way is healthy, it's fun, and it can help the participants cope with their present situation.

I don't remember ever observing another therapist using the question/answer song, nor do I claim to be the originator. Neither do I remember the exact time I began using this strategy. Some of the first songs of this type that I used in my practice employed questions that required a simple answer, i.e., "Who is your favorite president?" or "Who is your favorite movie star?" I was surprised that answers for these questions were quite difficult for some of the participants, because in general they seem to be pretty alert. I would sing a song for each participant that said, "My favorite president is _____." At the time I didn't seem to mind that everyone would not sing, because I was content to be in what I would describe as a "quasi-performance" mode. Unfortunately, I was surely overlooking some of the wonderful derivatives that can occur when one makes music therapy the primary focus, while saving the "dog and pony show" for another audience.

There was a breakthrough that occurred somewhat by accident. One of the group members asked permission to tell a story. He told about a sign that had been placed on the bulletin board in the facility that said "HAVE A GREAT DAY." Later on someone crossed through the word "HAVE" and inserted "MAKE." What a great story—what a great message. I was able to improvise the following song: "You've got to make—make a great day. You've got to make—make a great day. In everything you do and say, you've got to make—make a great day." Each person was asked, "What will you do to make it a great day?" Suddenly, it was appropriate to ask everyone to sing, because the song was for everyone—not personalized for an individual.

These are the steps to presenting the song:

1. Pass out a set of claves to each person. Having an instrument that requires two hands to play is important for total involvement. You will encounter persons who can only use one hand because of a stroke or other disability. Most of these persons have already devised a method for doing things that usually require two hands.

2. The question/answer song is presented one time by the therapist, and then everyone is encouraged to sing and play the claves. A "special instrument" (a hand-held that can be heard above the sound of the claves) is given to the person whose turn it is to answer the question.

Holidays and special seasons can provide ideas for songs that bring back personal memories. Try to avoid those questions that don't demand much creativity for an answer—things like, "What is your favorite food at Thanksgiving?" One song that explores the idea of "I Remember Halloween Long Ago" brought forth some good stories from the seniors. Still another had the basic theme of "This is What I Do." If songs can be about personal experiences, past and present, they will usually be very effective.

Eight | *The Closing Song*

Closing songs have been a part of music therapy sessions for as long as I can remember. Many organizations in our society have closing rituals at the end of the day, or at the end of a weekly meeting. Therapeutically, the closing is probably not high on the list of things that we do as music therapists, but it says to the participants, "We are finished now. Our time together has been well spent. We will meet again at a future date."

BASIC PARAMETERS

The closing song, being the last thing you do in a session, needs to have these characteristics:

1. It should be something in which everyone can participate in some way— probably singing, since passing out instruments takes time.

2. It should be very flexible in length, because you may be needing to leave for another appointment.

3. The contents may be flexible, because it is not an activity that we usually measure in terms of participation.

4. It may be the same song every week—giving participants a better chance to learn it.

5. It can be a slow song or a fast song. The former is recommended, since we probably don't want group members doing cartwheels or having wheelchair accidents afterward.

6. It may be a sacred song or a secular song, considering the makeup of the group and the philosophy of the facility.

SUGGESTED SONGS

My personal favorite and one that is dear to the hearts of most seniors is "Happy Trails" by Dale Evans Rogers (1951). Even though many seniors know the words, I usually pass out word sheets printed in large font.

If it is acceptable in the setting, I recommend my song called "God Be With You." The words and the tune (in the Appendix) are very accessible. The lyrics are as follows.

God Be With You

> *God be with you. God be with you.*
> *God be with you 'till we meet again.*
> *God be with you. God be with you.*
> *God be with you 'till we meet again.*
> *A—men, A—men, A—men, A—men,*
> *A—men, A————men.*

[Joseph Pinson © 1980]

In 1940 Woody Guthrie wrote a song called "So Long, It's Been Good to Know You." I have adapted the lyrics to say:

> *So long, it's time to get going.*
> *So long, it's time to get going.*
> *So long, it's time to get going.*
> *We've made some good music and had some fun,*
> *but it's time to be rolling along.*

In 1967 Willie Nelson recorded a song that he wrote called "The Party's Over." It was used by the NFL football for a while in its broadcasts. One of the men I encountered in a nursing home recommended it to me as a closing song, but I haven't quite come up with a way to alter the lyrics. I suppose the first line "Turn out the lights" could become "Pack up the stuff," but I haven't gone beyond that point in my thinking. It may be an idea that is useful to someone.

While I was writing this I thought about the tune for "Mary Had A Little Lamb" and thought it might become "Now it's time to say goodbye, say goodbye, say goodbye. Now it's time to say goodbye—time to move along." I decided that it would work for children but not for seniors.

Carol Burnett's farewell song "I'm So Glad We Had This Time Together" is a nice one that seniors have heard, but it is more of a personal statement, rather than one that everyone could sing.

There's a song I wrote for an individual in my studio that has the following lyric.

Goodbye Song #1

It's time to say "goodbye,"
It's time to say "so long."
It's time to say "see ya later—alligator."
It's time to say "farewell."

[Joseph Pinson © 1980]

It was written because this person had a fascination with saying "goodbye" in other languages. He would search *The World Almanac* for additional ways to express this sentiment. At the conclusion of the part stated above, he would sing words like these to the same tune:

In Germany they say "auf wiedersehen."
In Russia they say "das vedonia."
In Italy they "arrivederci."
And in China they say "zia jian."

The first part might be good for seniors. I've never used it but think it may have some possibilities. The tune is in the Appendix.

ADDITIONS

When time permits one of these songs might be added as an extra individual recognition. This would be a final farewell from the therapist.

Thank You for Making Good Music

Thank you, George, for making good music.
Thank you, Sally, for making good music.
Thank you, Shirley, for making good music.
We've had some good times—here today.

[Joseph Pinson © 2012]

Repeat the song enough times to get around to each person in the group. If you find yourself finishing in the middle of the song, just sing "Thank you—for making good music" until time for the final phrase.

A similar added song that might even be used with group participation is just the basic "bye-bye".

Goodbye Song #2

> Bye-bye, George. Bye-bye, Sally.
> Bye-bye, Shirley. Bye-bye, Jim.
> Bye-bye, Frank. Bye-bye, Mary.
> Bye-bye-bye. Bye-bye-bye.

[Joseph Pinson © 2012]

If you run out of names in the middle of this one, you just another one or two "bye-bye-bye"s.

WHAT WOULD YOU SAY?

These comments probably belong in the chapter about songwriting, but I am going to put them here. Think about what you would like to hear the group sing as a closing song. Think about "keep it simple" and "less is usually more." Once you have a lyric that you like, make up a melody. You can do this, if you really think about it. Here is a suggested lyric.

We've Had a Good Time

> We've had a good time—making our music.
> We've had a good time—making our music.
> We've had a good time—making our music.
> But now it's time to say so long.

[Joseph Pinson © 2012]

FINAL COMMENTS

The closing song can have a sort of "leftover" feeling, if we don't treat is as an important part of each session. It should be a time of farewell, but, more than that, it should be a time of celebration for the music that we have created together.

To accomplish this you must keep your energy level high until the very end. Don't just go through the motions. Present the song in a way that the participants will leave the area wanting more, and if they do, you will have accomplished your mission.

SUMMARY OF CHAPTER 8

Closing songs have been a part of music therapy sessions for as long as I can remember. Therapeutically, the closing is probably not high on the list of things that we do as music therapists, but it says to the participants, "We are finished now. Our time together has been well spent. We will meet again at a future date."

The closing song, being the last thing you do in a session, needs to have these characteristics:

1. something in which everyone can participate

2. flexible in length

3. flexible in content, because there is usually no measurement

4. maybe the same song every week, giving more time for learning

5. slow or fast, but not too fast

6. sacred or secular, considering the needs of the group.

Suggested songs for closing include: "Happy Trails" by Dale Evans Rogers (1951); my own version of "God Be With You" (1980), if the seniors and the facility are okay with sacred songs; an adaptation of Woody Guthrie's "So Long, It's Been Good to Know You" with words that begin "So long, it's time to get going", Carol Burnett's farewell song "I'm So Glad We Had This Time Together," and my "Goodbye Songs #1 & #2" (in the Appendix).

When time permits the therapist may add a song that recognizes each individual. These include my "Thank You" and the basic "Bye-Bye-Bye" that also recognizes each person (both in the Appendix).

Think about what you would like to hear the group sing as a closing song. Think about "keep it simple" and "less is usually more." Once you have a lyric that you like, make up a melody. You can do this, if you really think about it. There is an example called "We've Had a Good Time" in the Appendix.

The closing song can have a sort of "leftover" feeling, if we don't treat is as an important part of each session. It should be a time of farewell, but, more than that, it should be a time of celebration for the music that we have created together. To accomplish this you must keep your energy level high until the very end.

Nine | Composing Your Own Songs

BEGINNING PREMISE

In my opinion no one can teach you how to write a song, but there are guidelines that can be explained. Most everyone has some natural song writing ability, because songs and music are a part of our culture. Young children make up songs as they play. As they grow into adults they are taught that it is not polite to break into song in public, and some of these skills are never further developed, if not lost forever.

So, what am I saying—that we should just let our kids "do whatever" in public, to the horror of all that witness this unbridled freedom? No, I'm suggesting that in the home environment we encourage creativity that would include making up songs about whatever suits their fancy. At the same time we teach them about the things that are expected in the world outside the home.

We may stop making up songs, but our minds are still full of the music that has been a part of our lives. For this reason some of these suggestions may be useful to you in tapping into some of your own creative ability that may have lain dormant for a few years.

The most important aspect of learning to write songs is practice. Charles Wesley wrote over 5000 hymns. Only about 20 are still in use. In the process of writing we learn what works and what doesn't—or to say it another way, we probably learn how *not* to write songs before we learn how *to* write them.

LYRIC FORM

In Chapter 7 there has been mention of two basic lyric forms that are useful for working with seniors—**A A B A** and **A A A B**. These are designations of the order of the lyrics. Children know these forms as "If You're Happy and You Know It,

Clap Your Hands" (AABA) and "Go, Tell Aunt Rhoady" (AAAB). Most seniors know these forms as "Jada, Jada—Jada Jada Jing Jing Jing" (AABA) and "Skip to My Lou" (AAAB).

I think that a lot of amateur songwriters, especially those with no formal training in music, probably don't think much about form when they write. Most professional songwriters, with a few exceptions, are very aware of form, and their products have shown proof of this in the musical marketplace.

There are a lot of other song forms in use, but for our purpose it is best to concentrate on these two, since our principal objective is to make our songs easy and accessible.

MELODIC FORM

Melodic form is rarely as simple as lyric form; however, there are traits of good melodies that make them more or less accessible. In the melody for "Jada" the first phrase is almost identical to the second, except that the first "A" ends in a full cadence (on the tonic chord), and the second "A" ends in a half cadence (on the dominant chord). The "B" section is new melodic material, and the last "A" section returns to the original melody.

In "Skip to My Lou" the first phrase "A" establishes a set of intervals that are repeated in the second "A" at a different pitch level (a musical sequence). The third "A" is the same as the first, and the last phrase "B" is new melodic material. These "tricks" of the musical trade make these melodies simple and accessible.

If the terms "cadence, tonic, dominant, interval, sequence" are new to you, don't feel totally left out of the songwriting process. As stated before, most everyone has some natural songwriting ability, because our minds allow us to imitate what we have heard and experienced. We learn to speak before we learn to write. The old saying that "there is nothing new under the sun" (Ecclesiastes 1:9) is, in a sense, very true. Our creative minds are constantly rearranging material that is already part of our being.

THE PROCESS

Most songs (but not all) begin with an idea. "If I Loved You" (Hammerstein 1945) states the thoughts of the male lead and moves the drama forward. "Five Foot Two, Eyes of Blue" (Mahoney 1914) is the first line in a description of a girlfriend.

The songwriter adds phrases that complement the original idea. If the phrases you add don't give additional information about the same subject, they are probably not what you need. Sometimes the phrases rhyme, and sometimes they don't. In "Five Foot Two, Eyes of Blue" you have internal rhyme within the phrase.

The beginning phrase and those that follow usually have some similar rhythmic characteristics, but not always.

Melody is usually added after the lyric is complete, but not always. Some lyric writers begin with a melody that fits the mood or the style that they are looking for, and then they begin looking for words that will fit. The melody known as "Aura Lee", an American Civil War song, was written by George Poulton in 1861. New words were added for Elvis Presley in 1956, and because of advance orders, it became a "gold" record for RCA before it was ever released.

WRITING A NEW SONG

We are going to go through the steps for writing a new song for seniors. If this is a new experience for you, please be patient. Remember that, as stated before, most everyone has some natural song writing ability. Even if your first song is just a chant with no melody, it might turn out to be something that is very useful for the senior population. Here are the steps we will follow.

Step one

We need an idea. What is a common source of frustration for seniors in nursing homes or other care facilities? Are they struggling with loss of independence, loss of memory, loss of identity, loss of control, or loss of meaningful friendships? Are they feeling lonely, depressed, helpless, overwhelmed, unwanted, or useless?

If we decide to focus on loneliness, what might members of the group say about that? "I'm all by myself now, and there is no one that I know who cares about me." "I miss conversations with my late spouse, and there is no one here whom I can talk to." "Watching television reminds me that my friends are either dead or far away, and I miss all the good times that we had together."

Step two

Reduce the idea to a set of words that summarizes the message. The statements in the preceding paragraph are all on target, but none of them sounds like the words to a song. Hank Williams (1948) wrote "I'm So Lonesome I Could Cry." I don't think we want to put it that way, because it is not our objective to suggest that crying about the problem is the best solution—although a good cry from time to time is sometimes useful. If time permits we might have the group sing Hank's song as an introduction to our question/answer song.

I am going to suggest these two short phrases: "I feel so lonely, and I don't know what to do." This combines loneliness and helplessness—two of the feelings we identified. As it stands, the lyric expresses some common feelings in the group, but it falls short of identifying the feelings as more than individual.

Step three

Add a perspective that will make group members realize that everyone in the group has these same feelings, and that a solution, or at least a step in the right direction, would be to share these feelings and work together for some resolution. I am going to suggest that we add this phase: "There must be others who feel the same way too." Our completed lyric looks like this:

> *I feel so lonely, and I don't know what to do.*
> *There must be others who feel the same way too.*

Step four

Put these words into one of the lyric forms that we have discussed. Either one (**AABA** or **AAAB**) would work, but I am going to suggest the latter, because I want each member of the group to have three phrases to express the feeling of loneliness before we offer another perspective. With this form in mind the completed lyric looks like this.

I Feel So Lonely

> **A** *I feel so lonely, and I don't know what to do.*
> **A** *I feel so lonely, and I don't know what to do.*
> **A** *I feel so lonely, and I don't know what to do.*
> **B** *There must be others who feel the same way too.*

[Joseph Pinson © 2012]

I decided to make "B" phrase rhyme with the "A" phrase. It is not necessary, but it makes the second phrase easier to sing and easier to remember.

Step five

Consider writing a melody for this lyric. As stated previously, a well-written lyric may be presented as a chant with no melody; however, in my opinion, the addition of melody will probably make the therapeutic intervention more effective.

If the reader does not know basic principles of music, the tune that you make up will be in your head. This is the way a lot of melodies begin, even for trained musicians. For some of these the training sometimes gets in the way of creativity. If I have a chord progression in mind as I begin writing a song, my melody will sometimes be driven by the harmony. It's not absolutely wrong, but it may not be the best way to write.

Begin by looking for a melody for the first "A" lyric phrase. Find one that seems to fit the words and in a range that is easy to sing. A melody may have the same rhythm as speech, but a more interesting melody probably has a unique rhythm of its own. To put it in the context of speech, decide how the rhythm of your melody will sound:

I feel—so—lonely, and I don't know what to do.

I feel so lone—ly, and I—don't know what—to do.

I feel, I feel, I feel—so lone—ly, and I don't know—,I don't know what to do.

In creative song writing words may always be repeated to achieve the desired results. Generally, this technique gives the song a more "happy" (or at least less serious) feel. This may not be what we want for our song about loneliness. You can see the melody that I chose in the Appendix.

Once you have your melody for the first "A" in mind, think about something similar for the second "A." As you develop your songwriting skills, you may want the second "A" to be at a different pitch level or to have a different harmonic cadence on the end. The third "A" can be the same as the first. For the "B" section a different melody would appropriate. It needs to have a feeling of conclusion, since this is where the song ends in the AAAB form.

Your melody may be presented without accompaniment. Just be sure that your presentation is consistent. If you sing the melody one way the first time and another way the second time, your audience of seniors will be confused about which one you want them to learn.

Step six

Add an accompaniment to your melody. Even though some studies have shown that melodies without accompaniment can be very effective, it is my personal belief that a good set of harmonies presented in a professional manner can add much to the experience of participants. In the Appendix I have included some songs that are recommended for a cappella presentation; however, most of them are written for use with accompaniment if available. These songs have two sets of chords—a "standard" set and a "basic" set. Professional music therapists should be able to use either one. If you are just beginning to play an instrument, the "basic" should be your choice. They are as follows:

These are basic first position guitar chords that can be easily learned by the average person with no musical training. I am not including chord diagrams here, because this information is readily available on the internet. Search "guitar instruction" and you will find numerous sites that will give you all of the information you need plus videos of folks wanting to teach you how to play.

If you decide to develop simple keyboard accompaniments, I recommend that you play the chords with the right hand in the middle of the instrument with these spellings (low to high) or (left to right):

E = *G#-B-E*   **A** = *A-C#-E*   **D** = *A-D-F#*   **G** = *G-B-D*   **C** = *G-C-E*

With the left hand play a bass tone (same as the name of the chord) at least an octave (eight scale tones) lower. Alternate the right and left hand to create rhythm patterns. For basic accompaniment the keyboard does not play melody. Just as the guitar, it only provides a background for the melody that you sing.

The chords are grouped in what I call "circle order" (separated by an interval of and ascending perfect fourth or a descending perfect fifth). This terminology may mean nothing to one who has not studied music, but, if you are a professional music therapist and do not understand what I am talking about, you should strive to learn more about this principle that is the foundation of chord progression. Chords are sometimes designated by numbers or numerals. In the order presented, the primary chords (**V—I—IV**) are on either side of the tonic chord (**I**) that is the name of the key. So, using primary chords (that allow you to play any of the "basic" accompaniments in the Appendix), you have access to these keys: A major, D major, and G major. I have not made any of these seventh chords, because addition of the seventh is not critical to performance of the songs.

If you learn these five chords, you will be able to accompany many songs for seniors (or any other population). You will also be a prime candidate for exploring and possibly learning the accordion, since the chord buttons on that instrument are arranged in "circle" order.

Learning chords may also generate new melodic ideas. It's amazing how just strumming one chord on the guitar can motivate some folks (especially children) to start singing. It somehow establishes a mood for creativity. If you are reading this book and have not already developed some instrumental skills, I encourage you to get a guitar or a keyboard, learn one chord, and get started on your new and wonderful experience with music. If you elect to try the autoharp or its electronic equivalents, the Omnichord and the Q-Chord, all you have to do is press the buttons.

ANOTHER WAY TO WRITE

If you have difficulty composing your own melodies, you might try writing a lyric to an existing melody, as I did in a previous chapter. Songs of this type are sometimes called "piggy-back." If we took the tune from "This Land Is Your Land" (Woody Guthrie 1940) and a modified version of our lyric, it would look something like this:

> *I feel so lonely. I don't know what to do.*
> *I feel so lonely. I don't know what to do.*
> *I feel so lonely. I don't know what to do.*
> *There must be others—who feel the same way too.*

You might decide to start with a familiar melody and write a lyric for it. In the Public Domain Information Project I found the old tune for "Let Me Call You Sweetheart" by Leo Friedman (1910) and I thought of these words that would probably apply to most seniors in nursing homes:

> *Let me stay in bed today. I just don't want to get out.*
> *Let me stay in bed today. I just don't want to get out.*
> *Let me stay in bed today. I just don't want to get out.*
> *I've got to keep on moving. I just can't lie here and pout.*

Staying in bed is a familiar behavior that most group members might not want to talk about, but when they hear everyone "singing the same old song," they will probably be willing to open up and share their thoughts. The message here is not going against any doctor's orders. These folks wouldn't be in the group, if the medical staff had told them to stay in bed.

When I was hospitalized awhile back for six weeks, I remember feeling very helpless, even though my physical condition did not prevent me from getting out of bed. The doctors told me to keep my leg elevated at all times to promote healing. All of my needs were being provided. Getting up just didn't seem to be necessary. I was wrong. My healing didn't really get into "high gear" until the day I realized that I could get up to go to the bathroom, get out of bed for meals, take a shower by myself, and even take a stroll down to the nurses' station. From this experience I know that helplessness can be learned, and it can also be unlearned.

Writing new lyrics for some songs may present problems—especially those tunes that have lyrics relating to Christianity or patriotism. It would probably not be a good idea to take the tune of "What a Friend We Have in Jesus" and change the lyrics to say "Take me back to see my home town—just to stop and look around." The intent of the original words would most likely get in the way. On the other hand, you could probably set any lyric idea to the tune of "When the Saints Go Marching In," because it has a life of its own outside the church (jazz bands, etc.).

Our lyrics must certainly follow the rules of the facility. I remember teaching another set of clientele to sing the old song called "It's a Good Day" by Peggy Lee and Dave Barbour (1947). In the original a line near the end says, "Take a deep breath, and throw away your pills"—not the kind of message you want to impart to persons who lack good judgment. I changed the line to say "Take a deep breath, and don't forget your pills."

If you are a person with little or no musical training, I hope that your reading this excites you as much as it does me in writing this information. I can see folks out there who never touched a musical instrument learning how to sing and accompany themselves, and I know that if this happens, lives will be changed (yours and those whom you serve).

SUMMARY OF CHAPTER 9

In my opinion no one can teach you how to write a song, but there are guidelines that can be explained. Most everyone has some natural song writing ability, because songs and music are a part of our culture.

The most important aspect of learning to write songs is practice. Charles Wesley wrote over 5000 hymns. Only about 20 are still in use. In the process of writing we learn what works and what doesn't—or to say it another way, we probably learn how not to write songs before we learn how to write them.

In Chapter 7 there has been mention of two basic lyric forms that are useful for working with seniors—**A A B A** and **A A A B**. These are designations of the order of the lyrics. There are a lot of other song forms in use, but for our purpose it is best to concentrate on these two, since our principal objective is to make our songs easy and accessible.

Melodic form is rarely as simple as lyric form; however, there are traits in good melodies that make them more or less accessible. Most everyone has some natural songwriting ability, because our minds allow us to imitate what we have heard and experienced. We learn to speak before we learn to write. The old saying that "there is nothing new under the sun" (Ecclesiastes 1:9) is, in a sense, very true. Our creative minds are constantly rearranging material that is already part of our being.

Most songs (but not all) begin with an idea. The songwriter adds phrases that complement the original idea. If the phrases you add don't give additional information about the same subject, they are probably not what you need. Sometimes the phrases rhyme, and sometimes they don't. The original phrase and those that are added usually have some similar rhythmic characteristics, but not always. Melody is usually added after the lyric is complete, but not always. Some lyric writers begin with a melody that fits the mood or the style that they are looking for, and then they begin looking for words that will fit.

These are the steps to follow as you write your own song:

1. Think of an idea—maybe a common source of frustration for seniors in nursing homes or other care facilities. If we decide to focus on loneliness, what might members of the group say about that?

2. Reduce the idea to a set of words that summarizes the message. I am going to suggest these two short phrases: "I feel so lonely, and I don't know what to do." This combines loneliness and helplessness—two feelings that are common to seniors in residential settings. As it stands, the lyric expresses some common feelings in the group, but it falls short of identifying the feelings as more than individual.

3. Add a perspective that will make group members realize that everyone in the group has these same feelings, and a solution, or at least a step in the right direction, would be to share these feelings and work together for some resolution. I am going to suggest that we add this phase: "There must be others who feel the same way too." Our completed lyric now says, "I feel so lonely, and I don't know what to do. There must be others who feel the same way too."

4. Put these words into one of the lyric forms that we have discussed, either AABA or AAAB. Either one would work, but I am going to suggest the latter.

5. Consider writing a melody for this lyric. If the reader does not know basic principles of music, the tune that you make up will be in your head. Begin by looking for a melody for the first "A" phrase—one that seems to fit the words and is in a range that is easy to sing. Once you have your melody for the first "A" in mind, think about something similar for the second "A." The third "A" can be the same as the first. For the "B" section a different melody would be appropriate. It needs to have a feeling of conclusion, since this is where the song ends.

6. Add an accompaniment to your melody. There are more detailed instructions about creating your own accompaniment in the body of the chapter.

If you have difficulty composing your own melodies, you might try writing a lyric to an existing melody. Songs of this type are sometimes called "piggy-back." Or, you might decide to start with a familiar melody and write a lyric for it. Writing new lyrics for some songs may present problems—especially those tunes that have lyrics relating to Christianity or patriotism. If you are a person with little or no musical training, I hope that your reading this excites you as much as it does me in writing this information.

Ten | Including the Fun Factor

FUN FACTOR DEFINED

I have said it before, and I will say it again: "If you are in the business of providing music therapy services and not having fun, find something else to do." This is not to say that everything we do is fun all of the time. There are the challenges that come from unusual behaviors, difficult physical environments, demands of travel and the time needed to improve our skills to keep abreast of the latest developments in the field. Even these challenges are made less stressful when our focus is on the music that is the foundation of our profession.

The "fun factor" means that our clientele usually have fun during music therapy sessions, if we provide our services in a professional manner. It manifests itself in the types of strategy that we plan, in the musicianship that we bring to the situation, and in our general attitude about life.

With regard to work with the senior population it is important to have an attitude of respect for these persons who have played significant roles in the preservation of the freedoms that we enjoy. I tell students that there are not many opportunities for music therapy in third world countries—not because there is no need, but because the climate of poverty and political turmoil is not conducive to the work that we do.

SENIORS ARE FUNNY FOLKS

Beyond the idea of respect, we need to realize that our seniors, with their extensive life experience, are fascinating people—and, more than that, they are FUNNY!

In one of my groups there was a woman whom I will call Sandra. She always arrived with a scowl on her face that seemed to say, "Oh, NO—the music therapist is here again!" After providing services for a few weeks, I learned to anticipate this greeting. As it turned out, she was a person with a great sense of humor who enjoyed "putting me on" in this manner. Before the end of each session she was smiling and participating in a grand way. During one session we talked about how it is easy for "us older folks" to forget things (our eye glasses, our wrist watches, our hats, etc.). I improvised a song that said:

> *Sometimes I forget my _____, and that's okay.*
> *Sometimes I forget my _____, and that's okay.*
> *I won't let this little slip—ruin a beautiful day.*
> *Sometimes I forget my _____, and that's okay.*

The intent of the song was to say that we all forget things, but such mistakes should not cause us great distress. In discussing forgetful moments with the group, one woman let us know that sometimes when she gets up in morning, she forgets to put on her clothes. We had a good laugh, and then I altered the song to say:

> *Sometimes I forget to put on my clothes—and that's NOT okay.*

After we finished the song, Sandra said, "What would you do, if we all showed up for music therapy with no clothes on?" I responded, "I would stay in the car." This grand lady lived well into her nineties, because she had a great sense of humor, and because she didn't look upon her confinement in the nursing home as a curse—just another phase of life that she intended to live to the fullest.

In another group we explored the idea of that one special day in one's life that stands out as significant. This is the song that I used.

One Special Day

> *There's one special day—that I remember well.*
> *There's one special day—that I remember well.*
> *It's a special story—I love to tell.*
> *There's one special day—that I remember well.*

> *[Joseph Pinson © 2012]*

Most responses were things like "the day I joined the Navy," "the day I met my husband," or "the day I gave birth to my son." When we came to one woman in the group, she said, "the day I left my husband." We all had a good laugh, and she was pleased. I don't think she meant to be funny, but her honesty gave us all a new perspective on things. This brings me to my first important rule about creating an environment where "fun" can happen.

HONESTY IS THE BEST POLICY

Always be honest with your clientele. This doesn't mean wearing all of your "stuff" on your shoulder. It just means letting them know when you are having a bad day and then letting them know how happy you are to be with them for another music therapy session. And as I stated before, if you are not really happy doing this wonderful work—you may need to look for another profession.

Do you have a good sense of humor? I certainly hope so, because the persons with whom music therapists work are known for presenting challenges that can test one's endurance. If you can find the humor in difficult circumstances, you will discover that your own level of stress is much easier to manage. A good sense of humor comes from the knowledge that, as human beings, we are all very much alike. As you look around you may be thinking, "I hope that I am nothing like that person." In reality you are probably assessing the individual on a first or brief impression, or, even if your "take" is based upon more extensive experience, your real knowledge of that person is very limited. There is the expression "walking in another person's shoes," and it sounds like it might be possible, but it is not. To really accomplish that we would have to know the person's innermost thoughts that include all life experience. This is my point: if you have a tendency to judge other people, even with some considerable knowledge, you may not be cut out for this profession, and your developing a good sense of humor about life in general may be in jeopardy.

I remember a session with seniors that involved the question, "What is there about you that we don't know?" It sounds pretty personal, but I explained that we wanted to know something positive (like your love of good books, your ability to crochet, your coin collection, etc.) that the group would enjoy hearing about. The song went like this.

There's Something about Me

> There's something about me that you don't know.
> There's something about me that you don't know.
> There's something you don't know, but I swear it's really so.
> There's something about me that you don't know.

> *[Joseph Pinson © 2012]*

Responses included things like "I used to fly a helicopter," "I love to read biographies," "I have a collection of seashells in my room." When the question was asked of one woman, she replied, "There are a lot of things about me that you don't know, and I'm not going to tell you about any of them." It was not the response I had hoped for, but it was her response, her choice. Making choices is important for one who gets that opportunity less and less often.

Sometimes it is good to remind seniors that laughter is good for the soul, and the ability to laugh at yourself is a trait that everyone should develop. There is a song about this. Here is the lyric:

I Can Laugh

> *I can laugh. (ha-ha-ha) I can laugh. (ha-ha-ha)*
> *Even when the joke's on me. (clap-clap-clap)*
> *I can laugh. (ha-ha-ha) I can laugh. (ha-ha-ha)*
> *Even when the joke's on me. (clap-clap-clap)*

[Joseph Pinson © 2012]

There are probably a lot of times when individuals in a nursing home are the object of a joke about their behavior. The ability to laugh at oneself is a valuable tool for survival.

The seniors, being the "fun" people that they are, will set a climate for us to thoroughly enjoy each session. All we have to do is to "tune in" to their enthusiasm, their honesty, sense of humor and love of life. It is obvious that every member of every senior group does not have these attitudes, but those persons are in the minority, and if we deliver our services effectively, they may "change their tune."

MAKE A JOYFUL NOISE

Always present your music in a "joyful" manner. This means that you must prepare and be comfortable with whatever you have on the agenda for each session. It doesn't mean that you never make a mistake—just that you acknowledge each slip with a smile and keep going without missing a beat. I was fortunate to get to see Dave Brubeck perform at the age of 88. He made a few slips in his solos, and in each case he acknowledged these with a grin, and kept going. The joy that you demonstrate in your music sets the tone for the session. It is one thing to say, "Let's all be happy." Anyone can do that. It is quite another thing to be able to express that happiness through the music that you present.

I mentioned previously that I have my music therapy students perform at a local open mic each semester, because I think it is a good experience for them. My interest in this "public exposure" has a long history. I have been doing the open mics myself for several years. It's not because I have a need for recognition, although locally I am pretty well-known for my songs about unusual topics. There are two reasons that I continue this exercise:

1. It gives me additional experience performing for very diverse audiences.

2. It fills a need that I have to perform, and it makes me less likely to use the music therapy session as a vehicle for performance.

If you have a need to perform, that is good because music is obviously a very important part of your life. Every music therapist should have an outlet for performance. If you are a professional musician, play as often as possible, but don't get your days and nights mixed up. Nearly every community has opportunities for participation in community bands, choruses, church choirs, and various ensembles.

LESS IS USUALLY MORE

Remember—it is not your job to show these old folks what a "hot shot" musician you are. It is your responsibility to present music in a way that will get them involved—in the singing, the playing, or whatever else you have planned.

So—what do I mean when I say "Less is usually more." I mean that we provide enough musical support for seniors to encourage participation but not so much that it gets in the way of their being fully involved. Most of the songs presented in this book may be used without accompaniment. I am one who thinks that effective accompaniment can add an extra dimension to the strategy, but the jury (music therapy researchers) has not yet reached consensus on this. When participants can begin to create their own accompaniments, a maximum level of participation is achieved.

"Less is usually more" also apples to the lyrics that we create for the question/answer song that will be discussed in more detail in chapter 7. Someone may say, "At one point in my life I owned a wonderful little dog named Clarence." It may be true, but it doesn't make a very good song lyric. Instead, we might sing "Once upon a time—I had a dog." But for a *group* to sing, even that makes no sense, because everyone in the group didn't have a dog. It becomes accessible and logical when we draft still another version that says, "Once upon a time—I had a pet." So, we have a first line—what about the rest of the song? Well, the rest of the song could be just three more repeats of that phrase—and that would work; however, let's not get carried away with this "less is usually more" thing. We will challenge the seniors with one more complimentary line, and our completed song will be like this.

Once Upon a Time

Once upon a time—I had a pet.
Once upon a time—I had a pet.

A great companion—who meant so much to me.
Once upon a time—I had a pet.

[Joseph Pinson © 2012]

Note that no gender is mentioned, and that I used the personal pronoun "who", because most pets are definitely part of the family. The third line does not rhyme with the others. In the A A B A form rhyme is not necessary.

In our motor strategies we keep it simple. I have heard a student say, "Now—when I say 'Skip to my Lou,' I want you to respond by clapping a quarter note, two eighth notes, and two more quarter notes." You probably wouldn't even say that to an audience of musicians. Rather, you might say, "I will sing 'Skip to my Lou,' and you clap your hands" (demonstrating the rhythm pattern). I recommend that you have *no* instructions at all ("less is usually more"). Just sing and demonstrate the rhythm pattern (that I would probably simplify to just three quarter notes, because, as you know by now, "less is usually more.")

WHO ARE YOU?

If you have difficulty with the attitude of "joy" that I am describing, there may be some unresolved issues in your own life that need to be addressed. It is not my purpose here to advise you about the availability of counseling, but I can say that until you are able to get your own life in order, you will have some difficulty helping others make progress in their areas of emotional need.

Do you make eye contact with everyone you meet on the street or in any other location (assuming they are looking your way)? Why would you not do that? When we were children, we were taught to never talk to strangers, and that was probably good advice. We are no longer children, and we are involved in a profession that *cares* for people—all people. You certainly don't have to speak to everyone you encounter, but a smile is in order. If you practice this on a daily basis, you will be surprised how many folks return the favor.

Do you really understand what it means to live in a free society? A healthy appreciation of that privilege should make you very happy indeed. If you are reading this and do not live in a free society, I hope and pray that your circumstances will change for the better. It is easy to take freedom for granted, but it is so much better to understand that great sacrifices were made to provide that freedom and, therefore, we should celebrate this gift. The seniors we serve, part of the "greatest generation," paved the way with hard work and loss of loved ones. They deserve to see that we appreciate the things they have given us.

SUMMARY OF CHAPTER 10

The "fun factor" means that our clientele usually have fun during music therapy sessions, if we provide our services in a professional manner. It manifests itself in the types of strategy that we plan, in the musicianship that we bring to the situation, and in our general attitude about life. It is important to have an attitude of respect for these persons who have played significant roles in the preservation of the freedoms that we enjoy.

Beyond the idea of respect, we need to realize that our seniors, with their extensive life experience, are fascinating people—and, more than that, they are FUNNY!

Always be honest with your clientele. This doesn't mean wearing all of your "stuff" on your shoulder. It just means letting them know when you are having a bad day and then letting them know how happy you are to be with them for another music therapy session. If you can find the humor in difficult circumstances, you will discover that your own level of stress is much easier to manage. A good sense of humor comes from the knowledge that, as human beings, we are all very much alike. If you have a tendency to judge other people, even with some considerable knowledge, you may not be cut out for this profession, and your developing a good sense of humor about life in general may be in jeopardy.

Always present your music in a "joyful" manner. This means that you must prepare and be comfortable with whatever you have on the agenda for each session. It is one thing to say, "Let's all be happy." Anyone can do that. It is quite another thing to be able to express that happiness through the music that you present. If you have a need to perform, that is good; because music is obviously a very important part of your life. Every music therapist should have an outlet for performance.

When I say, "Less is usually more," I mean that you provide enough musical support for seniors to encourage participation but not so much that it gets in the way of their being fully involved. It is your responsibility to present musical stimuli that are accessible and that invite them to be a part of the music making. If you do this, and if they respond (which they will), they will experience the "fun" that you were hoping for.

If you have difficulty with the attitude of "joy" that I am describing, there may be some unresolved issues in your own life that need to be addressed. Do you make eye contact with everyone you meet on the street or in any other location (assuming they are looking your way)? Do you really understand what it means to live in a free society? The seniors we serve, part of the "greatest generation," paved the way with hard work and loss of loved ones. They deserve to see that we can celebrate with joy the gifts that they have given us.

Eleven | Self-assessment and Conclusion

Some persons have great difficulty standing outside themselves and looking back to observe what is going on. This may be because of limited intellectual ability, illness affecting cognitive functioning, or just plain stubbornness. If you fall into one of these categories, this chapter may not be for you. It will be divided into the same categories as listed in the sample assessment in Chapter 2.

BACKGROUND INFORMATION

Who are you? Give yourself a brief history of your life. Include the good times and the bad times, the successes, the failures and the many friends and enemies you have acquired. Concentrate on the good times, the successes, and the friends. We never forget anything that has ever happened to us, but to live a healthy and productive life, we need to put all of the bad stuff on the highest shelf and leave it there. If the bad memories are on a lower shelf, we will be sorting through them frequently and wondering: "Why did this happen?" "How could I have made such a stupid mistake?" and the most unproductive question of all—"What if?"

The question "What if?" makes absolutely no sense whatsoever, but it is one that most folks have asked. So—just state the facts about your life, and concentrate on the good things.

For your background information to be useful in self-assessment, you must accept who you are, where you have been and what you have done. Persons with mental impairment seldom have difficulty with this, because they have no concept of what they might have been. For the average person self-acceptance is a continuing task, but one that can pay rich dividends.

PROFILE OF CURRENT MUSIC SKILLS

Listening

Are you a good listener—a really good listener? Do you recognize when someone is able to match pitch in different keys? Do you recognize a natural gift for repeating rhythm patterns? Do you recognize when an individual has perfect pitch? Do you hear inherent possibilities for adapted performance in music that you encounter? Do you understand what someone who cannot speak is saying? Do you sense when a person's speech is affected by the present environment?

Rationale: From the moment you meet a new candidate for music therapy services you must be listening to everything you hear—their speech, their silence, their singing, and their playing rhythm instruments. I don't remember encountering a senior with perfect pitch, but I am sure they are out there. There have been several persons in my groups who had more advanced rhythm skills. In time you will probably know whether what you are hearing is an honest representation of the person or one that is modified because of the new environment. Speech is sometimes affected by illness or lack of development. You must learn to interpret gestures and in some cases provide pictures for a yes/no response. Your ability to hear and retain musical ideas will be valuable in planning strategies for intervention.

Moving

Do you enjoy dancing? Do you feel uncomfortable dancing in front of other people? Do you sense inherent possibilities for movement in the music you encounter? Are you able to improvise movement to music? Are you able to detect the slightest movement in an individual who is paralyzed from the neck down? Are you able to sense when a person is capable of more movement than what you see in the present environment?

Rationale: You will probably not be encouraging seniors in the group to dance. Based upon my experience it is not recommended. It will be important for you to evaluate their capabilities regarding arm and leg movement from a seated position. You will need to evaluate those who have great physical limitations. Your knowledge of music and movement will allow you to plan motor strategies in which the participants can be successful.

Playing

Are you able to improvise accompaniments for singing on one or more instruments? Are you able to transpose these into other keys? Are you able to play songs from different musical genres? Are you comfortable in playing your instrument(s) in front of diverse audiences?

Rationale: With proper preparation one does not always have to improvise accompaniments, but having this ability means that you can change or modify strategies on the spot. The use of different keys to accommodate the limited vocal range of the group is important. There is a comfort level with seniors that is probably different from most, but they are generally friendly and forgiving.

Singing

Do you love to sing? Do you sing in the shower? (Not required.) Do you know how to motivate others to sing? Do you know the words to many different songs representing various genres? Are you able to read and sing unfamiliar melodies from printed music?

Rationale: A love of singing, even if you don't have the very best voice, is essential in our work. When members of the group see that you love to sing, your ability to motivate them to sing has just taken a giant step forward. It is important to have a good repertoire of songs that you can sing; however, in music therapy we don't usually take requests, except possibly in hospice and/or psych work. The iPod is a great resource in these situations; however, you should continue to build your song repertoire. Reading printed music is the best way to learn songs. A lot of the renditions posted on the internet are inaccurate.

PROFILE OF SKILLS OTHER THAN MUSIC

Motor skills

Are you able to move about successfully to make appointments on time in various locations? Are you able to carry all of your "stuff" to and from sessions in an efficient manner? Does your necessary travel cause significant stress-related problems for you?

Rationale: Making appointments at various locations is very much a part of the lives of many music therapists. Just remember that your visiting the seniors is much less complicated than loading all of them on an accessible bus to bring to you. Your instruments and materials should be organized in a way makes the job of moving trouble-free. If your travel causes you stress, you may need to look for ways to reduce that stress without taking medication. For ideas about this, network with others who may have faced this same situation.

Cognition

Are you a member of a music therapy association? Do you read the journals? Do you search the internet for relevant information? Do you network with others in the field? Do you present information about your work at regional and national conferences? Do you present information about your work to local organizations?

Rationale: Association membership has been declining—probably because of the cost, but the information and networking that is part of that affiliation is very valuable to your continuing to develop your role as a music therapist. Maintaining your certification is some motivation for staying in touch, but if that is your only motivation, you are probably not growing as a music therapist. Sharing your work with others means that you are proud of your accomplishments. Good self-esteem is critical in our business.

Communication skills

Do you maintain a good system of electronic communication? Do you read and respond to emails in a timely manner? Do you respond to phone calls in a timely manner? Have you written journal articles, books, or methods? Have you written and/or recorded songs? Are you able to write a good letter when needed? Are you comfortable speaking about music therapy before others? Do you sometimes find yourself monopolizing a conversation?

Rationale: We are a global society connected by wonderful avenues for staying in touch. Communication skills are extremely important for success in our field. Being "connected" in too many different ways may limit your ability to communicate effectively. Have you begun to see a relationship between your work and the many research articles and videos that are available? If you spend more time in social networking than you do in music therapy related communication, your priorities may need some adjustment. If you sometimes seem to do all of the talking, learn to listen more often.

Social-emotional skills

Do you have a lot of friends? Do you have a lot of enemies? Does the room seem to clear out whenever you enter? Do you think of some of your clientele as friends? Is your relationship with your family a healthy one? Are you a member of local organizations, i.e., churches, civic groups, etc.? Do you make friends with people who can help you or with people you may be able to help?

Rationale: Real friendship (not electronic) is very important. For you to deliver effective services to persons whose social skills are lacking, you must come to the table with a fairly secure set of your own social connections. It is not to say that everyone always has the friends that they want, nor does it mean that everyone has stable family connections. Regardless of your situation you must be secure in maintaining a set of friends who are there for you when you need them. If you are not a magnet for attracting others, then it is your job to seek out others to whom you can relate, with the hope of creating lasting friendships. You will find friends among those whom you serve, but these friendships do not extend beyond the therapy environment.

POSITIVE TRAITS

Just as in the sample assessment you will want to make a list of your positive traits. There are probably areas that are not fully developed, but if they are "on track," that is positive. Assess all areas of your life. If you are able to live within your means, that is positive. If you budget your time effectively, your chances for success are very good. If you stay abreast of the latest developments in the field, you are moving in the right direction. There are positive traits that we sometimes overlook, and it may be useful to talk to a friend who will be honest about this. Your list may include some of these:

1. A good set of skills on keyboard and/or guita.

2. A good network of other music therapist.

3. A good knowledge of seniors and their music.

4. A healthy self-respect and self-esteem.

5. A good knowledge about what is happening in the field.

6. A good connection with your community.

AREAS OF NEED

The other side of the ledger is sometimes more difficult to measure, because we tend to overlook or just not be aware of our shortcomings. I can remember as a young man thinking how great I was in some areas of music, only to learn that my competition was several steps ahead. Comparing your own abilities to others is seldom very useful, because everyone is different. As painful as it may be, asking a friend to give you some honest criticism may be a good way to learn more about yourself.

Your list may include some of these:

1. Skills on keyboard and/or guitar that need more development.

2. Lacking a connection with other music therapists.

3. Lacking knowledge of seniors and their music.

4. Lacking a healthy self-respect and self-esteem.

5. Lacking knowledge about what is happening in the field.

6. Lacking a good connection with your community.

RECOMMENDED INTERVENTION

You may get a handle on who you are and where you want to go, and that is good. The next step is to set goals and objectives for yourself that are realistic and attainable.

A *goal* is a direction of treatment. The goals that we set for the individuals whom we serve usually have no completion date. A date of completion may be useful for your purpose.

Let's suppose that you have decided to learn to play the guitar with more ease and flexibility. It's a goal that probably wouldn't take too long to accomplish, if you apply yourself to the task. Your goal might be stated like this:

> I will improve my guitar skills by this time in the next calendar year.

An *objective* is an immediate focus of treatment. For every goal you may have more than one objective. Your objectives should probably be:

1. I will find a good teacher and meet with that person every week.

2. I will take his/her suggestion about what instrument is best.

3. Once lessons have started, I will practice 30 minutes every day.

This plan of action, if followed consistently, will yield good results. Will you be the best guitar picker on the block? Probably not, but will you find great satisfaction in the progress that you have made? Absolutely!

CONCLUSION

We have explored providing group music therapy for seniors, from assessment through delivery of services. It is a growing field that will continue to employ music therapists, because, in spite of the advances in technology and medicine, there is still a lot of need among this population.

If you do the self-assessment and discover some areas that need improvement, it is time to draft some goals and objectives aimed at correcting those deficiencies.

An ideal model for seniors would be care in the home by family members, but this is rarely possible in today's fast moving society. Even when it is possible, there are often issues that arise that make quality of life very difficult. Music therapy is often the key to helping seniors and family members find peace in their shared struggle.

SUMMARY OF CHAPTER 11

Some persons have great difficulty standing outside themselves and looking back to observe what is going on. If you have this condition, this chapter may not be for you.

The self-assessment is based upon the same format that appears in Chapter 2. Begin with a brief history of your life. Include the good times and the bad times, the successes and the failures and the many friends and enemies you have acquired. For your background information to be useful in self-assessment, you must accept who are, where you have been and what you have done.

In your *profile of music skills* you should assess:

1. *Listening*: including the ability to recognize good music traits in your clientele and hearing inherent possibilities for adapted performance in music that you encounter.

2. *Moving*: including the ability to sense inherent possibilities for movement in the music you encounter and the ability to sense when a person is capable of more movement than you see in the present environment.

3. *Playing*: including your ability to improvise instrumental accompaniments, transposing these into other keys, and your comfort level playing your instrument(s) in is front of diverse audiences.

4. *Singing*: including your ability to motivate others to sing, knowing the words to many different songs, and your ability to read and sing unfamiliar melodies from printed music.

In your *profile of skills other than music* you should assess:

1. *Motor skills*: your ability to move about successfully to make appointments on time, your ability to transport your equipment efficiently, and whether travel causes significant stress.

2. *Cognition*: your ability to network with other music therapists, to stay abreast of recent trends in the field, and to present information about your work at regional and national conferences.

3. *Communication skills*: your ability to maintain a good system of electronic communication, to write letters and respond to emails in a timely manner, and to be able to speak comfortably about music therapy in public.

4. *Social-emotional skills*: your ability to have a good set of friends, to have a healthy relationship with your family, and to maintain contacts in the community.

Under the category of *positive traits* you will list things like good skills on keyboard and/or guitar, a good network of other music therapists, a good knowledge of seniors and their music, a healthy self-respect and self-esteem, a good knowledge about what is happening in the field, and a good connection with your community.

Under the category of *areas of need* you will list instrumental skills that require more development, lack of connection with other music therapists, lack of knowledge of seniors and their music, lack of a healthy self-respect and self-esteem, lack of knowledge about what is happening in the field, and a lack of a good connection with your community.

Under the category of *recommended intervention* you will develop a set of goals and objectives to assist you in making positive progress in your areas of need.

This chapter concludes by saying that services to seniors is a growing field that will continue to employ music therapists, because, in spite of the advances in technology and medicine, there is still a lot of need among this population. Music therapy is often a key to helping seniors and their families achieve a better quality life.

Appendix

Songs for Seniors in Group Music Therapy

Basic Hello Song #1

sing without accompaniment

Joseph Pinson, ASCAP

Hel - lo! (clap-clap) Hel - lo! (clap-clap) Jim-my is here. (clap-clap-clap)

Hel - lo! (clap - clap) Hel - lo! (clap - clap) Jim-my is here. (clap - clap - clap)

Hel - lo, Hel - lo, Hel - lo, Hel - lo! Jim-my is here. (clap - clap - clap)

Basic Hello Song #2

Joseph Pinson, ASCAP

Hel - lo San - dra. (clap - clap - clap) Hel - lo San - dra. (clap - clap - clap)

Hel - lo San - dra. (clap - clap - clap) Hel - lo San - dra. (clap - clap - clap)

We're so glad, so glad, so glad you're here to - day. (clap - clap - clap)

As in all songs that use a person's name the rhythm must be adjusted to fit the accents in pronunciation. We pronounce "Arlene" with the accent on the first syllable; therefore, we would not begin her name on a strong beat. "Ar" goes on a weak beat; "lene" on a strong beat. This seems like a simple thing, but I hear it done wrong quite often.

Big Cheer Song

Joseph Pinson, ASCAP

Whenever you see blank measures in a song, these are places where extra rhythm activity may occur (clapping, playing instruments, etc.), as noted in the text. As in other songs that use a person's name, it is important to change the rhythm to fit the accent of the name. A name like "Anastasia" would need to begin with two eighth notes before the downbeat of the first measure of each phrase. A name like "Jennifer" would begin on the downbeat, but the notation would be two eighth notes followed by a half note.

Everyone is Different

Joseph Pinson, ASCAP

This song could be used in a lot of different ways. The question could be "What is different about you?" After each individual response have the entire group sing the song. The example in the text talks about the "art gallery"—a set of prints of paintings. Let each person choose one and describe what it means to him/her. The question could be "What is your favorite food?" (one that I usually avoid)—but it still has some possibilities helping seniors get to know one another.

God Be With You

Joseph Pinson, ASCAP

Goodbye Song #1

Goodbye Song #2

Greeting Song

Joseph Pinson, ASCAP

With handbells or hand-held chimes. Participant may use one or two.

With limited rhythmic clapping (or claves). May want to add this later.

This one may begin with singing only. As participants become more familiar with the song, the therapist may add chimes or bells—or the rhythmic clapping or claves.

I Can Laugh

Joseph Pinson, ASCAP

Seniors (and all of us) make a lot of mistakes. It can be very embarrassing. The ability to laugh at oneself is a valuable tool in maintaining quality of life.

I Feel So Lonely

Joseph Pinson, ASCAP

In the text we discussed writing a melody for this lyric. You will notice that the melody for the second phrase is similar to that of the first phrase, but it is stated a step higher. For the third phrase I went back to the first melody and modified it slightly towards the end. The last phrase is different from the first three, and its rhythm (longer notes on "must be") gives a stronger feeling to the conclusion.

As I stated before, we learn to write songs by writing. If this is new for you, I encourage you to try as many new ideas as possible. Write them down. Re-work them, and then re-work them again.

I Expect Respect

Score

Joseph Pinson, ASCAP

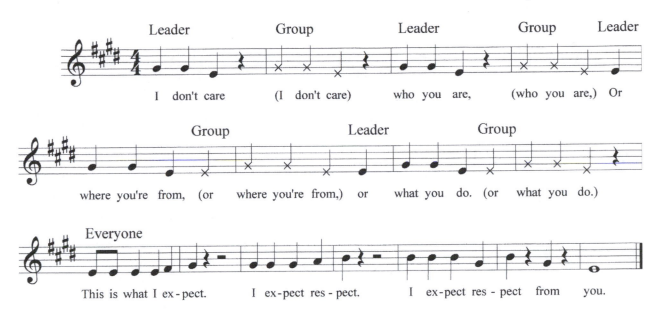

Certainly, people living in nursing homes know about not getting enough respect. It is not that staff persons are not dedicated, caring individuals—just overwhelmed with the demands of their jobs that require serving many different needs simultaneously.

No chords are given in the song. It could be harmonized, and I have done that on occasion, but I feel that it is most effectively presented in one of the following ways:

1. As a chant—with no melody and no chords. Use claves and a special instrument for the person who answers the question.

2. Sing with a very simple keyboard or guitar accompaniment—playing the same chord on the quarter note beat throughout the song. Participants use claves and a special instrument for the person answering the question.

3. Allowing person answering the question to strum an open tuned guitar (from lowest to highest string: E B E G# B E). Others in the group play claves.

4. Allow person answering the question to play E and G# (representing the E chord) on hand-held chimes. Others in group play claves.

I Remember Halloween Long Ago

Joseph Pinson, ASCAP

The question is "What do you remember about Halloween when you were young?" You may want to offer a few suggestions like "trick or treat" or "dressing in home-made costumes" or "bobbing for apples." All participants play claves. The special instrument may be castanets with handles for a "bone-cracking" sound or offering a microphone to each individual for the opportunity to make a ghost sound.

I Will Find a Way

Joseph Pinson, ASCAP

Certainly, every senior in residential care has this feeling from time to time. The purpose of the song is to allow them to acknowledge that feeling and to learn that others share their concern. The music therapist will remind that all we really have to "get through" is the next second, the next minute and the next hour—until the day is complete. The question might be "What will you do to help yourself and others make it through the day?" This idea will be reinforced with the special instrument (G5 and G6 hand-held chimes or a large handbell (G4 or G5) struck with a mallet). The person who has just been the focus of discussion plays this instrument at the fermati in the score. The therapist will provide a cue when it is time to play. Timing is flexible.

In My Merry Oldsmobile

Edwards & Bryan, 1908
arr. Joseph Pinson, ASCAP

Original

Come a way with me Lu - cile in my mer - ry Olds - mo - bile. Down the

road of life we'll fly. Au - to - mo bub - bling you and I. To the

church we'll swift - ly steal. Then our wed - ding bells will peal. You can

go as far as you like with me in my mer - ry Olds - mo - bile.

Meter Conversion

Come a - way (clap-clap) with me (clap-clap) Lu - cile, (clap-clap - clap) In my

mer - (clap-clap) ry Olds-(clap-clap) mo - bile. (clap-clap - clap) Down the road (clap-clap) of

life (clap-clap) we'll fly. (clap-clap - clap) Au - to - mo bub - bling (clap-clap) you and (clap-clap)

I. (clap-clap-clap) To the church (clap-clap) we'll swift-(clap-clap) ly steal. (clap-clap-clap) Then our

wed-(clap-clap) ding bells (clap-clap) will peal. (clap-clap-clap) You can go (clap-clap) as far as you

like (clap-clap) with me in my mer-(clap-clap) ry Olds-(clap-clap) mo - bile. (clap-clap-clap)

It's Good to See You

Joseph Pinson, ASCAP

In the first version the chord changes cover the rhythmic gaps in the melody. The second version with the basic chords would probably be done best without accompaniment. The therapist would cue the persons in the group to let them know when to clap.

The seniors should be encouraged to sing and clap every time the song is played.

Let Me Call You Sweetheart

Friedman & Whitson, 1910
arr. Joseph Pinson, ASCAP

The second version of the song is probably best led without accompaniment in order that the therapist can cue instruments (with his/her hand clapping).

Make a Great Day

Joseph Pinson, ASCAP

This song came from a story that a group member offered. There was a sign on the bulletin board that said "HAVE A GREAT DAY." Someone crossed out the word "HAVE" and inserted "MAKE." We talked about the things that each person could do to "make a great day." This song was improvised on the spot and has become a favorite in groups that I have done since that time. Each person in the group plays claves. As each person answers the question, he/she plays a "special instrument" (something that will sound above the claves).

My Best Friend

Joseph Pinson, ASCAP

The "best friend" may be described as a person who is living or who is no longer alive. Someone might even name a pet. Some may have difficulty making a choice, of "best," but there is usually one who stands out. And, yes, "means" is present tense. The person or pet may be gone, but the good memories remain.

Now Hear This

Joseph Pinson, ASCAP

This song is designed for the modified bull horn—that used to be available in toy stores. There are probably some variations on the internet. When you speak into it, it makes crazy inaudible sounds. This allows the person using it to say whatever is on his/her mind—without being understood by anyone in the group. I usually have the group sing the song first. When I give the bull horn to someone, I will play another chorus while they do their thing. This can be time consuming, but the song is short, so it is not likely to go over your budgeted amount of time.

One Special Day

Joseph Pinson, ASCAP

When you go over the question, give some examples, like "the day you met your husband," "the day you joined the army," or "the day your son was born." The memories of seniors are enhanced when we give them suggestions. If you simply say "What was the best day of your life?" that is a very large category that makes an intelligent response more difficult.

Shake Hands

Joseph Pinson, ASCAP

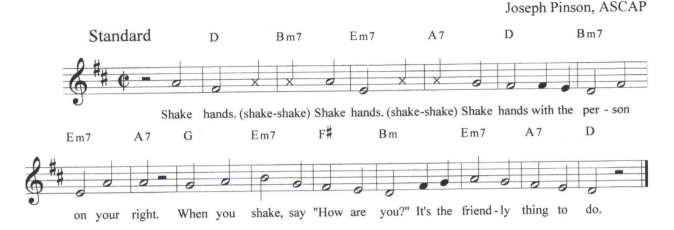

If the therapist is working alone, he/she may have to do this one without accompaniment. If there is an aide nearby that could participate in the hand shaking, then the therapist could accompany the song. Because of the length of most music therapy sessions, you may not have time for this one; however, if one of your objectives is for all members of the group to shake hands at each meeting, then this is the song that will serve as your measurement tool.

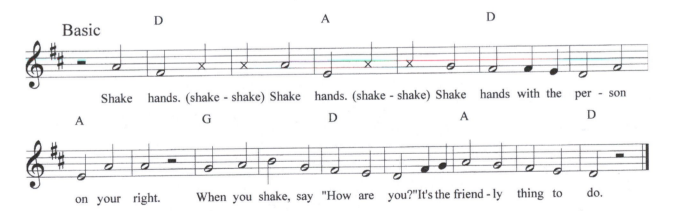

As stated before, the music therapist will act as song leader/facilitator on this one. We are not asking the participants to sing—just shake hands and say "How are you?" It seems like a small thing, but anything we can do to begin to build a bridge between members of the group, especially those who may be strangers, is well worth the effort.

Take Me Out to the Ball Game

VonTilzer & Norworth, 1908
arr. Joseph Pinson, ASCAP

Thank You for Making Good Music

Joseph Pinson, ASCAP

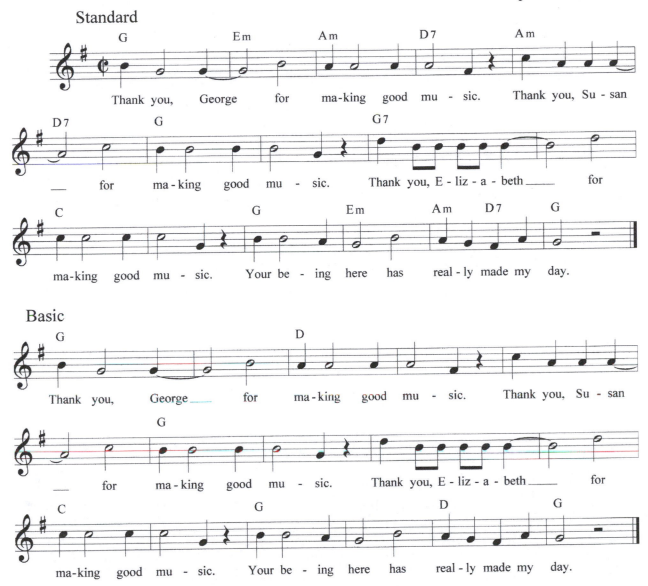

For each person named in the song the rhythm of the melody needs to be adjusted to fit the accents of his/her name. This is something that you should learn to do in the moment, because you will not know ahead of time who is attending and what the order of the group will be. If you run out of names in the middle of the song, just sing another phrase or two saying "Thank you for making good music" and end with the concluding phrase.

There's Something about Me

Joseph Pinson, ASCAP

The question used in this song is "Can you tell us something positive about you that we don't know?" Answers can be from the past or the present and might include things like "I like to knit" or "I used to live in New York City." All participants sing and play claves. The person answering the question plays a special instrument that can be heard above the claves. The therapist may have to ask questions that require only a "yes" or "no" response, such as "Do you enjoy reading?" or "Did you play sports in high school?"

This is What I Do

(to the tune of *This Little Light of Mine*)

arr. Pinson

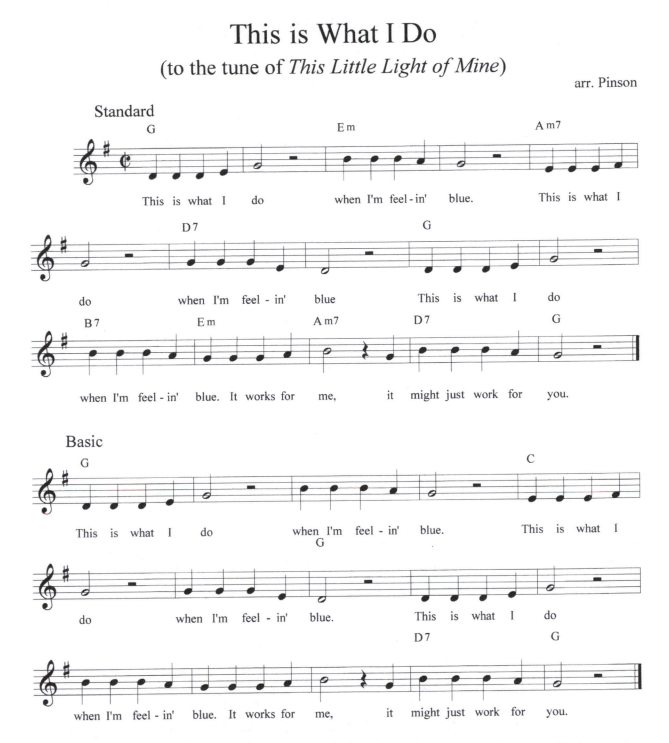

In presenting this song I don't normally mention its original name. If the seniors recognize it and ask about the origin, I will tell them; otherwise, I just let them enjoy the experience without bringing in too much history that is not relevant to the question. A song that uses new words to a familiar melody is sometimes called a "piggyback" song.

We're Glad You're Here

Standard

Joseph Pinson, ASCAP

Basic

It is important to change the rhythm patterns to accomodate different names. "John is" would be two half notes. "Penelope is" would become an eighth note pick-up followed by two eighth notes, a half note and a quarter note. The accented notes (on strong beats of the measure) should correspond to the way we say a person's name. This song may be presented without accompaniment, allowing the therapist to devote full time to leading the singing and the clapping.

We're So Glad You're Here

Joseph Pinson, ASCAP

We've Had a Good Time

Joseph Pinson, ASCAP

If you are approaching these songs from the "basic" chords, I encourage you to explore the "standard" chords when time permits. You will find that in many instances they move in "circle" order (up a perfect fourth and down a perfect fifth). Learning this type of chord motion is one of the keys to improving your harmonization. This song seems like a fitting conclusion to this book. I've had a good time writing it, and I hope you have a good time using what is here.

References

Altschuler, I. (1948) "A Psychiatrist's Experiences with Music as a Therapeutic Agent." In D. Schullian and N. Schoen (eds) *Music in Medicine*. New York: Henry Schuman.

Belgrave, M., Darrow, A.A., Walworth, D., and Wlodarczyk, N. (2011) *Music Therapy and Geriatric Populations*. Silver Spring, MD: American Music Therapy Association.

Cevasco, A.M. and Grant, R.E. (2003) "Comparisons for different methods for eliciting exercise-to-music for clients with Alzheimer's disease." *Journal of Music Therapy 40*, 41–56.

Coffman, D. D. (2002) "Music and quality of life in older adults." *Psychomusicology 18*, 76–88.

Cohen, A., Bailey, B., and Nilsson, T. (2002) "The importance of music to seniors." *Psychomusicology 18*, 89–102.

Holmes, C., Knights, A., Dean, C., Hodkinson, S., and Hopkins, V. (2006) "Keep music live: Music and the alleviation of apathy in dementia subjects." *International Psychogeriatrics 18*, 4, 623–630.

Michel, D. and Pinson, J. (2005, 2012) *Music Therapy in Principle and Practice*. Springfield, IL: Charles C. Thomas.

National Nursing Home Survey (2004) *Current Resident Tables*. Atlanta, GA: CDC/National Center for Health Statistics. Available at www.cdc.gov/nchs/nnhs/nnhs_products.htm, accessed on May 25, 2012.

Pinson, J. (1989) "The music in my heart is for you." Official song of the American Music Therapy Association—Southwestern Region. Unpublished song.

Public Domain Information Project. Available at www.pdinfo.com/PD-Music-Genres/PD-Popular-Songs.php, accessed on May 18, 2012.

United States Census Bureau (2010) *2010 Census of Population and Housing: 2010 Summary File 1*. Available at www.census.gov/prod/cen2010/doc/sf1.pdf, accessed on May 20, 2012.

Watkins, G. (1997) "Music therapy: Proposed physiological mechanisms and clinical implications." *Clinical Nurse Specialist 11*, 2: 43–50.

Wigram, T. and Gold, C. (2006) "Music therapy in the assessment and treatment of autistic spectrum disorder: Clinical application and research evidence." *Child: Care, Health and Development 32*, 5, 535–542.

World Health Organization (2011) *Summary: World Report on Disability*. Geneva: WHO. Available at http://whqlibdoc.who.int/hq/2011/WHO_NMH_VIP_11.01_eng.pdf, accessed on May 12, 2012.

Further Reading

Clair, A. A. and Memmott, J. (2008) *Therapeutic Uses of Music with Older Adults*. Silver Spring, MD: American Music Therapy Association.

Douglass, D. (1985) *Accent on Rhythm: Music Activities for the Aged* (3rd ed.). St. Louis, MO: MMB Music.

Gregory, D. (2002) "Music listening for maintaining attention of older adults with cognitive impairments." *Journal of Music Therapy 39*, 244–264.

Hanser, S. (1990). "A music therapy strategy for depressed older adults in the community." *Journal of Applied Gerontology 9*, 283–298.

Hudakova, A. and Hornakova, A. (2011) "Mobility and quality of life in elderly and geriatric patients." *International Journal of Nursing and Midwifery 3*, 7, 81–85.

Jacobs, D. (1988) *Who Wrote That Song?* White Hall, VA: Betterway Publications.

Johnson, G., Otto, D., and Clair, A. A. (2001) "The effect of instrumental and vocal music on the adherence to a physical rehabilitation exercise program with persons who are elderly." *Journal of Music Therapy 38*, 82–96.

Karras, B. and Hansen, S. T. (2005) *Journey through the 20th Century: Activities for Reminiscing and Discussion*. Mt. Airy, MD: Eldersong.

Krout, R. E. (2006). "Music listening to facilitate relaxation and promote wellness: Integrated aspects of our neurophysiological responses to music." *The Arts in Psychotherapy 34*, 134–141.

Pelletier, C. L. (2004) "The effect of music on decreasing arousal due to stress: A meta-analysis." *Journal of Music Therapy 41*, 192–214.

Wylie, M. E. (1990) "A comparison of the effects of old familiar songs, antique objects, historical summaries, and general questions on the reminiscence of nursing home residents." *Journal of Music Therapy 27*, 2–12.

Index

Group and Individual Work with Older People
A Practical Guide to Running Successful Activity-based Programmes
Swee Hong Chia, Julie Heathcote and Jane Marie Hibberd
Illustrated by Andy Hibberd
Paperback: £18.99 / $29.95
ISBN: 978 1 84905 128 6
208 pages

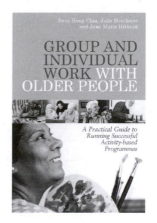

Being active is fundamental to a person's sense of physical and mental wellbeing, and the need to engage in purposeful and meaningful activity does not diminish with age. However, common effects of ageing, such as reduced vision and hearing, arthritis, dementia, and in some cases social isolation, can affect an older person's ability to participate in therapeutic and recreational activities.

Introducing the concept of PIE (Planning, Implementation and Evaluation), this practical resource will enable professionals working with older people to initiate and run successful activity-based programmes with their clients, either individually or in groups. The authors guide the reader through the processes of group and individual work, and provide step-by-step instructions for a range of activities, including arts and crafts, music, drama, movement, relaxation, reminiscence, and day-to-day tasks such as taking care of personal hygiene and preparing food and drinks. The book also describes the importance of assessing and evaluating activity-based work, with examples of completed evaluation and assessment forms. Useful case studies and self-reflective activities for the facilitator are included throughout.

This book will be an invaluable for occupational therapists, creative arts therapists, health and social care practitioners and all other professionals working with older people.

Contents: Introduction. 1. Quality of Life in Older Age. 2. Group and Individual Work. 3. Communicating with Older People. 4. The Importance of Using Assessment when Working with Older People. 5. Task Analysis: Working Step by Step. 6. Initiating and Creating a Group. 7. How to Facilitate Art and Craft Activities with Groups and Individuals. 8. How to Facilitate Music and Drama Activities with Groups and Individuals. 9. How to Facilitate Movement and Relaxation with Groups and Individuals. 10. How to Facilitate Reminiscing with Groups and Individuals. 11. How to Facilitate Life Skills Using Group and Individual Work within a Supported Living Session. 12. How to Facilitate Cognitive Based Activities for Stimulation with Groups and Individuals. 13. How to Facilitate a Carer Support Group. 14. The Importance of Evaluating Work with Older People. References. Index.

Swee Hong Chia is a lecturer in Occupational Therapy at the University of East Anglia, UK. He has extensive experience of teaching the theoretical aspects of groups and using groups to maintain or facilitate change with people of all ages who have developmental disabilities and cognitive difficulties. **Julie Heathcote** is an Alzheimer's Society Approved trainer for reminiscence work. She has extensive practical experience of working with groups of older people and of training carers, support workers and volunteers to use these approaches when working with older people individually and in groups. **Jane Marie Hibberd** is a lecturer in Occupational Therapy at the University of East Anglia, UK. She specialises in working with older people, and has experience of using groups in a therapeutic context with this client group. Jane also facilitated the Activity Coordinators Networking Group in Cambridge, UK.

Connecting through Music with People with Dementia
A Guide for Caregivers
Robin Rio
Paperback: £14.99 / $23.95
ISBN: 978 1 84310 905 1
144 pages

For people with dementia, the world can become a lonely and isolated place. Music has long been a vital instrument in transcending cognitive issues; bringing people together, and allowing a person to live in the moment. Connecting through Music with People with Dementia explains how a caregiver can learn to use melody or rhythm to connect with someone who may be otherwise non-responsive, and how memories can be stimulated by music that resonates with a part of someone's past.

This user-friendly book demonstrates how even simple sounds and movements can engage people with dementia, promoting relaxation and enjoyment. All that's needed to succeed is a love of music, and a desire to gain greater communication and more meaningful interaction with people with dementia. The book provides practical advice on using music with people with dementia, and includes a songbook suggesting a range of popular song choices and a chapter focusing on the importance of caregivers looking after themselves as well as the people they care for.

Suitable for both family and professional caregivers with no former experience of music therapy, and for music therapy students and entry level professionals, this accessible book will lay bare the secrets of music therapy to all.

Contents: Preface. 1. Introduction. 2. All You Need to Know About Music. 3. Singing and Choosing Songs. 4. Making a Connection. 5. Putting What You Know to Use. 6. Stimulating and Relaxing Music Choices. 7. Memory and Associations. 8. Caring for Yourself. Songs. References Appendix: Song List, Recording Artists and Resources

Robin Rio is a board certified Music Therapist and Associate Professor at Arizona State University, USA.

Group Music Activities for Adults with Intellectual and Developmental Disabilities
Maria Ramey

Paperback: £24.99 / $39.95
ISBN: 978 1 84905 857 5
176 pages

Musical games and activities can significantly improve the social, emotional, cognitive and motor skills of adults with intellectual and developmental disabilities. However, many music therapy resources are written with children in mind, and it can be difficult to find suitable age-appropriate activity ideas for adults.

This versatile collection of 100 group music activities is the perfect sourcebook to provide insight to music therapists who are new to working with this client group, and inspiration to those familiar with working with adults but in need of fresh ideas. Each activity is developed in depth, with clear goals and instructions, and includes easy adaptations to suit a wide range of ability levels. With accompanying CD and sheet music, this book contains a ready supply of lively and original songs that can be used by practitioners of all musical abilities.

With this practical and inspiring resource, music therapists, caregivers and other professionals working with adults with developmental and cognitive disorders will never be short of age-appropriate ideas again.

Contents: Acknowledgements. Preface. Music Therapy with Adults with Intellectual and Developmental Disabilities. How to Use This Book. Activities. 1. Play the Tambourine. 2. Smile and Wave. 3. I Like to Sing. 4. Let's All Play Together. 5. Scarf Dance. 6. I'm In the Mood. 7. Weekend Song. 8. My Sunshine. 9. Triangle Teams. 10. Shaking to the Music Beat. 11. Live Music Relaxation. 12. Shake Up High. 13. Visual Lyric Analysis. 14. Cluster Drumming. 15. Pick A Card: Instruments. 16. Frame Drum Imagination. 17. Heartbeat. 18. Over the Rainbow. 19. I Love…. 20. Old MacDonald Had A Band. 21. Clap Your Hands, One Two Three. 22. I Feel Good. 23. Matching Loud and Soft. 24. Just For Fun. 25. Paint the Air. 26. Howl At the Moon. 27. Twelve Days. 28. Random Duet. 29. Emotion Connection. 30. Stretchy Band Hokey Pokey. 31. Concerto Soloist. 32. Conducting. 33. Guess the Hidden Instrument. 34. How Many Beats? 35. Walkin' Down the Street. 36. Walk Like the Music. 37. Visual CDs. 38. Pick A Card: Feelings. 39. Jump and Jive. 40. Mirroring. 41. Twist. 42. Follow My Beat. 43. My Favorite Things. 44. Cha Cha Cha. 45. Signs of the Seasons. 46. Manic Monday. 47. News From Home. 48. Traveling Places. 49. Colors Everywhere. 50. Nature Box. 51. This Is Me. 52. Wave the Scarves. 53. Shake A Question. 54. Guess That Sound. 55. Clap Your Hands to the Music. 56. Move to the Music. 57. Dance Conducting. 58. Marching In. 59. Song Bingo. 60. Musical Ball. 61. Musical Feelings. 62. Party Animal. 63. Celebration Song. 64. Drum Q&A. 65. Rhythm Sticks Alphabet. 66. Your Story Through A Song. 67. Five Letter Favorites. 68. Boom Boom. 69. I Won't Back Down. 70. Leadership: African Drumming. 71. Marching Band. 72. Eye Choose You. 73. What I Like About You. 74. I Can See Clearly now. 75. Xylophone Conversation. 76. Boomwhacker Beat. 77. The Music Comes Over. 78. You Are. 79. Collective Mandala. 80. Turn, Turn, Turn. 81. Simple Songwriting. 82. Musical Shapes. 83. Animal Adventure. 84. Do-Re-Mi Chimes. 85. Roll Your Fists Around. 86. Rhythm Shakers. 87. Rhythmic Hot Potato. 88. Shake, Rattle and Roll. 89. Film Scoring. 90. Musical Charades. 91. Collaborative Drawing. 92. Color to the Instruments. 93. Musical Board Game. 94. Guitar Strum. 95. Rhythm Pies. 96. Music Listening Game. 97. Index Card Songwriting. 98. Chordal Songwriting. 99. Xylophone Ensemble. 100. Creative Singalongs. Appendices. Appendix A: Sheet Music for Original Songs. Appendix B: List of Books Illustrating Well Known Songs. Appendix C: List of Songs Referred to In Activities. Appendix D: Supply Resources. Appendix E: Contributors. Appendix F: Activities Listed By Goal Area. Appendix G: CD Track Listing. References.

Maria Ramey is a music therapist at Hope University in California, a non-profit fine arts school for adults with developmental disabilities. She provides group therapy sessions to clients with varying degrees of developmental and cognitive disabilities, ranging in age from 22 to 72. In addition she provides private music therapy sessions to clients with various disabilities and illnesses. She resides in Anaheim, California with her husband and three children.